INTRODUCTION

AF333549

It is paramount that one study about Islam from books written by Muslims. This book is intended for those who have little or no background in Islam. The material is intended for children, however, we are all children at certain levels of knowledge in a variety of subjects. It is my belief that this book can be used by students from age twelve to fifty.

Before beginning your reading of this book, you should turn to the Appendix and follow directions. This pretest will inform you of your knowledge of the basic principles of Islam.

I wish to give my thanks to the Muslims Student Association of the United States and Canada for permission to use their material for this book. After learning the material in this book, you might wish to learn more about Islam. An excellent source for further reading is: Islamic Book Service, 10900 W. Washington Street; Indianapolis, Indiana 46231

Cover Illustration of Grand Mosque in Tombouctou. Courtesy Hotel Azali.

Photography by Howard Smith.
Combined Edition
First Printing, 1984
Second Printing, 1985

IBSN# 0-913811-01-7
LC# TX1-292-506

CONTENTS

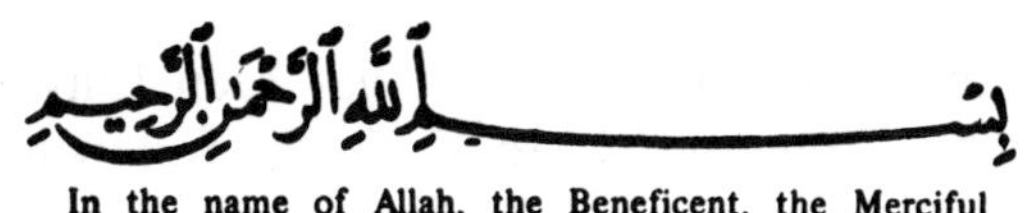

1. INTRODUCTION

Islam teaches that there is only One God, who is called Allah in Arabic. He has created all and is above all things in the universe and on earth, and there is no one and nothing which is like Him or can be compared to Him. God loves us, and for our guidance and benefit has sent his commandments and laws through persons specially chosen by Him who are called prophets or messengers of God.

Since the time of the emergence of the first man on this earth, God in His mercy has raised from among men numerous prophets or messengers, such as Abraham, Isaac, Jacob, Joseph, Moses, David and Jesus. The last of all the messengers was Muhammad (peace be on them all).

Islam is not a new religion. It consists of the same basic message which God has given in all true religions, and all prophets brought this same message for our guidance. Muhammad (peace be on him), the Last Prophet of God, taught us the full and complete meaning of Islam — surrender and commitment to the will of God — through his words, his actions and the revealed Book, the Holy Qur'an. We are fortunate to be believers in the Last Prophet of God, for Muhammad (peace be on him) is the bearer of the message of peace and submission to God.

The life history of Prophet Muhammad is very important, for his words, his deeds and his character are the highest example we can follow. It is also the history of great struggle and great achievement. This history is so complete and well-documented that there cannot be any doubt whatsoever about its accuracy and authenticity, for it has been fully preserved within the light of recorded history. In the following sections we will present the life story of the Prophet in its various stages.

2. THE BIRTH OF MUHAMMAD (PEACE BE ON HIM)

Muhammad was born in Mecca, Arabia, on 12 Rabi Awwal 54 years before *Hijra,* or Monday, August 20, 570 A.C., early in the morning. The Holy Qur'an says: "And say, the truth has come and falsehood vanished; surely the falsehood is ever bound to vanish." This applies very well to the life of the Prophet himself, and we can remember his birthday as a day of blessing and rejoicing for all mankind.

3. CHILDHOOD

Muhammad's father Abdullah died six months before his birth, and his gentle mother Amina died when he was hardly six years old. Thus Muhammad· (peace be on him) was left without the love of a mother or father very early in life; but he was always the beloved of God. He came of a very noble family, the Banu Hashim branch of the Quraish tribe. This greatest and noblest of the children of Arabia was taken care of first after his mother's death by his grandfather Abdul-Muttalib, but he too died just two years after the death of Muhammad's mother. Next the young Muhammad was taken in by Abu Talib, his poor uncle. Now here in the deserts of Arabia was an orphan without the care of a father, the love of a mother, brother or sister. But God had chosen him out of all mankind to be His messenger to save humanity from sin and destruction.

4. YOUTH

Muhammad (peace be on him) spent his youth as a trader helping his uncle Abu Talib who ran caravans of goods from one place to another. Muhammad traveled to Syria twice trading with these caravans. He was willing to do any honest work, and

2

sometimes he even herded sheep. He was never ashamed of any job he did, no matter how humble. He used to mend his clothes and shoes himself. He thus established the dignity of any honest labor.

5. CONDITION OF SOCIETY BEFORE THE PROPHET'S MISSION

From his childhood, Muhammad (peace be on him) was deeply distressed by the corrupt society of Arabia. His people spent their time and energy in drinking and gambling. . Arab society at that time was hopelessly divided because each family or tribe was concerned only with its own interests, engaging in frequent wars with one another at even the slightest excuse. This constant tribal warfare saddened Muhammad, for he felt that his people should all be one family and behave like brothers to each other. Like most of the world in the Seventh Century, the Arab people neither respected their women nor loved their daughters. Girls were so unwanted that often girl babies were buried alive by their fathers at birth. Ka'aba, the most sacred place of worship of God, first founded long ago by the Prophet Abraham, was now the home of 360 idols, one for each day of the year. It disturbed Muhammad that this sacred place was so abused. It was one of the darkest periods for all of human society, for even Christianity and Judaism had become ineffective and confused. Muhammad was grieved at these conditions and wanted somehow to improve them.

6. THE CHARACTER OF THE PROPHET

The time had come when the world once again needed God's mercy and guidance, and the best of all men, Muhammad (peace be on him) was chosen by God to bring His message once again to a lost humanity. God selected for His messenger the one man in this corrupt society who kept himself clean and pure, merciful, tolerant and righteous, and who remained the worshipper of the One Supreme Being.

Muhammad (peace be on him) meditated and thought of God in the Cave of Hira, a hill near Mecca, where he used to go very often. Even in that corrupt society where virtue was not necessarily admired nor sought after, Muhammad was always known and respected by his acquaintances for his high moral standards, and people used to call him *al-Amin,* the Trustworthy One.

7. MUHAMMAD'S MARRIAGE

Among the many merchants who hired Muhammad (peace be on him) to take charge of their caravans of goods was a lady named Khadijah. Khadijah was twice widowed, had two sons and a daughter by her two previous husbands, and was successful in her inherited business. Moreover, Khadijah was forty years old while Muhammad was twenty-five. Since Muhammad was poor and illiterate as well, he hardly seems like a logical choice for a wealthy woman of noble family like Khadijah. But through her business dealings with Muhammad, she had seen that he was honest, kind, responsible and virtuous in every way, a man of rare qualities. She could see the great worth of Muhammad, a worth far greater than any money could buy, and she humbly asked him to marry her. As God knows all things to come, He knew the tremendous hardships and trials which were to come to the Prophet. Only God could know that Khadijah would be the first to accept Islam and that she would encourage, help and sustain Muhammad in the troubled times ahead, when she was his greatest source of human support.

Muhammad (peace be on him) and Khadijah enjoyed a successful, happy marriage for the next twenty-five years until Khadijah's death. They had three sons, all of whom died in infancy, and four daughters, who all survived. Khadijah was Muhammad's only wife as long as she lived. She died when he was about fifty years old, or ten years after he began his prophetic mission. Khadijah had helped and supported her husband in every way she could through the hardest years of his mission. He never forgot her love and support, for he called her the "blessed among women" and remembered her lovingly all through the remainder of his life.

After Khadijah's death, years later, Muhammad (peace be on him) married several times. But all his wives except one —

4

'Aisha — were either widows or divorced. They needed him rather than his needing them. Some of the marriages were for the purpose of cementing friendship among the various warring tribes and others were to give support to the widows of his Companions. But whether the reason for the marriage was political or charitable, Muhammad treated all his wives with love, respect, fairness and kindness. He thus taught a world which treated women little better than animals to love and respect all women — rich or poor, young or old, educated or illitereate, widowed or divorced. He said to this world, "Heaven lies under the feet of the mother."

8. MUHAMMAD AS PROPHET

Muhammad (peace be on him), when he retired to the Cave of Hira from time to time, used to ponder over the basic questions about man, the universe, its Creator, and man's relationship to Him. He could not believe that there were many gods, each having charge of a certain part of the world or of man's life, nor could he believe that gods made of wood or stone — idols made man's own hands — could have the slightest power over men's affairs. To God, the only Supreme and Powerful One, Muhammad directed his meditation and his worship.

One night in the month of Ramadan — "The Night of Power and Excellence" (*Lailat ul-Qadr*) — when Muhammad (peace be on him), then in his fortieth year, was meditating in the Cave of Hira over the ultimate realities, he heard a mighty voice twice ordering him: "Read" (*Iqraa*). Muhammad was frightened and overawed, and finally he answered the voice, saying, "I cannot read." But the order was repeated until at last Muhammad tremblingly asked, "What shall I read?" The voice came:

"Read, in the name of your Lord, Who created –
Created man from a clot!
Read, for your Lord is Most Bountiful,
Who taught be means of the pen,
Taught man what he does not know." (Qur'an 96:1-5)

This was the first revelation of the Qur'an, brought by the Angel Gabriel.

Muhammad (peace be on him), shaking with fear, immediately rushed home and told his wife Khadijah what had happened. She lovingly reassured him, saying that it could not have been anything harmful to him, for as he was an upright man God would protect him. A little later Khadijah was the first person to embrace Islam.

Shortly after this first revelation, God revealed to Muhammad (peace be on him), through the Angel Gabriel, that he was chosen to spread God's message and to show misled humanity the right path. He now quietly began his mission, preaching the Oneness of God, the path of submission to Him, the folly of idolatry, and the inevitable coming of the Day of Judgment when each human being would have to give an accounting of his deeds before God. Religion in those times had become a matter of belief only, but Islam proclaimed without any qualification that belief without action is meaningless and ineffective.

The Qur'an declares the Oneness of God in these words:

"Say: God is One, Unique;
God, the Source (of everything);
He has not fathered anything nor is He fathered;
And there is nothing comparable to Him." (*Surah* 112)

This message, though simple and basic, was the greates possible challenge and threat to the idol-worshippers of Mecca. They did not wish to change their ways of living and they were afraid of losing their power if idolatry was given up, so they began to insult and humiliate Muhammad (peace be on him) in the most cruel and persistent manner. But nothing can really harm one who is protected by God.

9. PREACHING AND OPPOSITION

Muhammad (peace be on him) patiently and quietly started preaching to friends and family members. This period of preaching lasted for three years, and the total number of people who embraced Islam during this time was less than thirty. Among them were Khadijah, 'Ali (Muhammad's cousin and ward), Zaid (a slave who had been freed by Muhammad, as slavery and equality cannot go hand in hand), Abu Bakr, 'Uthman and Talha (Muhammad's close friends and life-long companions).

After three years, God's command came to preach openly. Muhammad (peace be on him) then went up on the mount of Safa near Mecca and declared the Oneness of God, warning the Meccans of God's judgment. He invited them to believe and to act on this belief by following God's commandments and living righteous lives. This infuriated the Meccans, for such a message threatened to destroy all their power and all the interest they had vested in the idols of Ka'aba. They threatened him with dire conequences if he did not cease his open preaching. As if in answer to their threats, a few days later the Prophet went to Ka'aba and declared: "There is no deity but God, and Muhammad is His Messenger."

The non-believers were even more startled and disturbed. Threatening had failed, so now they tried to bribe him with riches, honor, women and even kingship. Muhammad's simple answer to this was: "If they place the sun on my one hand and the moon on the other, even then I shall not desist from performing my sacred mission."

Since both bribery and threats had failed, the non-believers now began the most cruel persecution of Muhammad and his followers, whose only "crime" was that they believed in One God, avoided evil, practiced goodness, kindness, justice, love and brotherhood. Some of these Muslims, such as Bilal, 'Ammar and Khabbab were thrown on the burning desert sand in the heat of the sun and heavy stones were laid on their chests. Other Muslims were dragged through the streets at the end of a rope. Some were beaten so mercilessly that they died.

The non-believers of the Quraish could not subject Muhammad (peace be on him) to the worst of these tortures because he belonged to the Banu Hashim family and any such treatment would have started an unending civil war. A forty years' war had just ended and they could not afford another war so soon. But Muhammad did not altogether escape physical torture. It was the daily custom of the Meccans to throw rubbish on him and they strewed thorns in his path. On one occasion when our beloved Prophet went to Taif, a nearby town, to preach the message of God, he was mercilessly attacked and stoned by the people. He was so badly hurt that he almost fainted. While suffering these tortures, Prophet Muhammad would only say, "O God, show them the right path because they do not understand." Thus did he carry out his mission as the bringer of peace and love to all mankind.

For five years the sufferings of the Muslims multiplied day by day. In spite of these trials, however, more persons joined the believers each day. About eighty Muslims migrated to Abyssinia, where they were pursued by the unvelieving Quraish; but the Muslims escaped unharmed. In the sixth year of the Prophet's mission, two very important persons embraced Islam: Hamza and 'Umar. 'Umar's conversion is a landmark in the history of Islam, for 'Umar immediately started praying in Ka'aba. It was a great challenge, which infuriated and alarmed the Quraish. They now increased their persecution of the Muslims still further, but still more and more people embraced Islam.

10. THE BOYCOTT

The Quraish had tried threats, bribes and torture to no avail. They decided that they must deal with Muhammad (peace be on him) directly, but when they asked his family to hand him over to them, the Banu Hashim would not give him up. As a result, the Banu Hashim was obliged to flee to a nearby hillock known as *Shu'ab-Abu Talib*. Here they were forced to live for three years. The Quraish boycotted the Banu Hashim completely. They were often without food and were forced to scavenge for themselves. Sometimes they had to live on the roots and leaves of trees. At times the Prophet and others with him had to cook and chew on their leather shoes because there was nothing else with which to satisfy the pangs of hunger. Clothing too had become very scarce.

But soon after this Abu Talib, the Prophet's uncle, and Khadijah, his beloved wife, his two greatest supporters, died.

The Quraish, now finding Muhammad (peace be on him) left
without this support, increased their persecutions.

11. HOPE

By this time the people of the city of Medina, who used to
visit Mecca each year, had heard of the Prophet's message.
Many of them embraced Islam and they urged the Prophet to
come to Medina, sincerely pledging to stand by him at the cost
of their lives if necessary. This promise seemed the only ray of
hope, through the mercy of God, in those darkest days.

12. ME'RAJ OR ASCENSION

At this time the Holy Prophet (peace be on him) was
honored by God Most High in a most beneficent and glorious
manner. God showed him all that was in heaven and the universe
in a vision. He met all the earlier prophets and led them in
prayer. He saw the Glory and the Light of God. This was the
greatest favor that God could bestow upon any human being.
The Prophet received forgiveness for sinners if they repent and
do good. Five daily prayers and fasting were ordained by God at
this time. This most radiant vision, physical as well as spiritual,
is known as *Me'raj*, which means "having reached the highest
point," or as the "Vision of Ascension." It gave strength to the
Prophet at the darkest moment of his mission when he most
needed it.

13. HIJRAT OR EMIGRATION

It was in the thirteenth year after the Prophet (peace be on
him) received the Message that the Quraish became desperate
enough to decide to assassinate him and end his mission permanently. In order to protect themselves from the revenge of
the Banu Hashim family, assassins were chosen from each of the
different tribes so that no single tribe alone would bear the
responsibility, for of course the Banu Hashim would not be
able to fight all the tribes at one time. But God revealed their

evil design to the Prophet, and he was able to escape unharmed.

On the night the Quraish planned to murder the Prophet (peace be on him), when the house was surrounded by the assassins, Muhammad asked his cousin Ali to lie down in his bed. Muhammad, even at the time of gravest danger, was careful to confide to Ali's care all the things which had been entrusted to him by different persons, to be returned to their owners. This is a great example to us of honoring the trust and faith which had been placed in him by persons who were, in fact, mostly non-believers. The Prophet slipped out of his house, passing among the waiting assassins, but by the grace of God, they were caught by a strange sleep so that they did not see him going through. Later the assassins observed Muhammad's bed, and seeing a person sleeping in it, they assumed that it was the Prophet. When they finally discovered that it was Ali instead of the Prophet, they were beside themselves with anger and frustration. The Holy Prophet, with his trusted friend Abu Bakr, was by then well on the way to Medina.

An alarm was sounded, and the Quraish went in pursuit of the Prophet (peace be on him). The two hunted men traveled during the night but went into the Cave of Thaur when day broke to rest and also to hide from their outraged pursuers. A party of the Quraish reached the mouth of the cave in their search, but the cave seemed so utterly abandoned that they could not imagine that anyone might be there and did not even enter it. Abu Bakr was despondent and apprehensive in those critical moments, but the Prophet told him, "Have no fear, for God is with us" (9:40). Those who believe in God's mercy need never be afraid nor lose confidence, for God is the Best and Strongest Protector.

The Quraish offered a reward of a hundred camels to anyone who captured Muhammad (peace be on him) dead or alive. Thereupon many people went to search for him for the sake of the reward as well as out of motives of revenge; but no one could harm the Prophet, for one whom God protects needs no other protection, and the two companions reached Medina safely. The Qur'an, referring to this emigration, says:

"...They [the unbelievers] made their plans, and God also made plans, but the best of planners is God." (8:30)

10

14. ISLAMIC CALENDAR

The Islamic calendar starts from the year in which Muhammad (peace be on him) emigrated from Mecca to Medina. It starts from 1 Muharram in the year of the *Hijra*, or July 15, 622 A.C. Great actions are more important in life than the date of birth or death. The Muslim era, therefore, does not start with the Prophet's birth date but with the most significant event in the history of Islam, for this date marked a turning point in the success and spread of Islam.

15. THE MUSLIM COMMUNITY IN MEDINA

When the Prophet (peace be on him) and Abu Bakr arrived in Medina, they were welcomed with great joy by the Muslims, both the Medinites and the many emigrants from Mecca, who, prior to the Prophet's departure, had slipped away with their families to Medina. All the people of Medina were eager to have the Prophet come to live with them. In order that no one would feel slighted, the Prophet allowed his camel free reign to go where it would through the city. Guided, perhaps, by the God of all Creation, the camel stopped and began to graze on a piece of vacant land owned by two orphan brothers. Here, then, the Prophet decided to remain, and paying the brothers for the land, built the first mosque of Islam with a small house for himself attached. In the future, this and all other mosques were not only places of worship of God but also a shelter for the homeless and travelers 1 a meeting place to discuss public affairs.

The first need was to provide for the emigrants from Mecca. These Muslims had left behind them in Mecca almost everything they possessed and were in great need of help until they found a means of livelihood and homes in their adopted city. The Muslims of Medina, who received the title *"Ansar"* (helpers), shared everything they had with their emigrant Muslim brothers who had forsaken family ties, homes and property for the sake of God's religion, and through this expression of brotherhood the lives of the two groups were welded into one community.

The Prophet (peace be on him) and his people were now

safe from the continuous persecutions of the Quraish; for although the unbelievers were still determined to wipe out him and his community, they were too far away (200 miles) to be anything like the threat they had been in Mecca. In Medina the mission of the Prophet entered into its second and final phase, that of an organizer of a community based on the Divine law. While the revelations he received at Mecca were primarily concerned with matters of faith, the revelations which were given to the Prophet at Medina cover a broad range dealing with all aspects of human conduct, pertaining to food and drink, marriage and family life, morals and manners, trade and commerce, peace and war, crime and punishment. It should be borne in mind that the specific and general injunctions revealed to the Prophet are for all time, but his companions were the first to hear them and put them into practice. Previously it had not been possible to organize the Muslim community as a social group very effectively because of all the difficulties which the Quraish inflicted upon it, but now the Prophet set about to create an Islamic society composed of the community of individual Muslims. The religion of Islam is not only a belief, nor is it merely a personal observance. It is a way of life for the individual and for the community, and every aspect of life is bound by its laws and practices. A good community makes good individuals, and good individuals in turn make a good community, each receiving its strength from the other.

While the Muslims were welded together into a solid brotherhood by their common belief and the way of life which it brought to them, they still were threatened by the enemies of Islam. There were, both among them and among outlying tribes as well, people who wished evil to the Muslims and who tried in every way — even through treachery and collusion with the Quraish — to destroy them. Against these discontented people the Muslim community had to be on constant guard, and at times measures had to be taken to deal with them. In addition, from time to time the Quraish, burning with the determination to snuff out the people of truth and righteousness, brought their armies to fight the Muslims. In 2 A.H. (After *Hijra*), a strong, well-armed Quraishite force of 1000 men started toward Medina. They were met at Badr by an ill-armed, hastily gathered group of about 300 Muslims. The Quraish had numbers and arms plus planning, but the Muslims had God's help, and the Quraish were routed. This victory gave moral and spiritual support to the Muslims and crushed the hope of the Quraish temporarily. But about a year later they again advanced on Medina to destroy the Muslims. This time they were victorious in battle, but the Muslims were able in the end to turn them back. This encounter is called the Battle of Uhud. Later the Quraish army surrounded Median and held it under seige for several weeks. Supplies and water were cut off from the Muslims, and they suffered so severely from lack of food that they tied stones to their stomachs to stifle the pangs of hunger, but still they held out against the much stronger force which was laid out against them. God was with the Muslims, and in the end the Quraish withdrew.

The spirit of the Muslims was so strong that they held their own lives to be of small account and gladly laid them down in the cause of Islam. God had ordered them to fight so that justice and right might prevail, and they answered His call with the last ounce of their strength and resources. This striving in the cause of Islam is called *Jihad. Jihad* means striving in the cause of God, but it has a much broader meaning than only fighting in battle. It means to strive, with one's time, energy, possessions, talents and with all the resources of one's life, for God.

Although toward the end of his life the Prophet (peace be on him) was the head of a large nation, still his way of life was extremely simple and austere. At times he and his household lacked even basic necessities. In all his words and deeds he was a living example of the teaching of Islam, drawing men and fixing their hearts firmly on God through his teaching and his perfect upright life. We are fortunate that many of his sayings and his actions have been recorded through his companions in the collections called *Hadith* or the Traditions of the Prophet to serve as a guide to us.

16. RE-ENTRY INTO MECCA

In 7 A.H. a treaty, known as the Treaty of Hudaibiya, was

signed with the Quraish, who had now begun to be afraid of the strength of the Muslims. Under its terms, the Prophet (peace be on him) and his followers went to Mecca to perform the pilgrimage (*Hajj*) to God's Sacred House, Ka'aba. In 8 A.H., however, the Quraish violated the treaty and it was terminated. The Prophet, with a large number of Muslims, set out for Mecca to end the hostility of the Quraish permanently, without shedding blood if possible. The Quraish, seeing that resistance was now impossible, gave in, and the Prophet and his followers entered the city where he had first announced God's Message without bloodshed. He entered Ka'aba and pulled down the idols which had so long desecrated the house of worship of the One God, who has no partner.

The Prophet's enemies, who had persecuted him and his followers relentlessly for so long, were now at his mercy, awaiting punishment. When the Prophet (peace be on him) had humbly thanked God for the success which had been granted to the Muslims, he asked the frightened people of Mecca, "What do you think I am going to do to you?" They anxiously replied, "O noble brother and son of a noble brother, only goodness." The Prophet who came with the Message of mercy and salvation to all the world answered them: "No blame is on you this day. Go to your homes, for you are all free." Thus the Prophet underlined for all Muslims to come how to treat a fallen enemy.

By 10 A.H. most of the people of Arabia, including many Jews and Christians, had become Muslims. Even those who did not accept Islam lived in peace, safety and protection, for the Qur'an clearly says, "There is no compulsion in the matter of faith" (2:257).

17. THE LAST PILGRIMAGE

Prophet Muhammad (peace be on him) performed his last pilgrimage (*Hajj*) in 10 A.H. Although it had not been quite twenty-four years since he began his mission, there was now a band of 114,000 Muslims to accompany him to Mecca. No other prophet had been granted such a miracle of success. Only eleven years earlier, the Prophet had been driven out of Mecca, a hunted man with a price on his head; now he has the leader of the whole of Arabia.

The Last *Khutba* (sermon) which the Prophet delivered on this occasion was the fulfillment of his mission. He emphasized the Oneness of God, the sacredness of the Message, the coming of the Day of Judgment, respect for women and the sanctity of life and property, saying, "Know that all Muslims are brothers to one another. You are one brotherhood. I have left with you that which, if you take hold of and follow, your affairs will not go wrong, namely, the Book of God and the Practice of His Messenger..." At this time he received almost the last revelation from God:

> "This day have I perfected your religion for you and completed My favor upon you, and have chosen for you Islam as your religion." (5:4)

18. THE DEATH OF THE PROPHET

The Prophet (peace be on him) fell ill and, after rallying briefly, grew steadily worse, his strength failing rapidly. At noon on Monday, 12 Rabi Awwal, 11 A.H. (June 8, 632 A.C.), while he was praying earnestly in a whisper, the spirit of the Last Prophet took flight to the "blessed Companionship on high."

> " '...To God we belong, and to Him is our return.' " (2:156)

The people of Medina were grief-stricken. 'Umar, a companion of the Prophet (peace be on him), was so overcome with grief that he refused to accept the fact of the Prophet's death. He went into the mosque, where many were praying and the word of the Prophet's death was on every tongue, and declared, "I will kill anyone who says that the Prophet is dead!" Because 'Umar was close to the Prophet and an important man among them, the Muslims were frightened and bewildred at that difficult moment. Chaos and confusion gripped them until a word from Abu Bakr brought them back to the way of Islam: "If you worshipped Muhammad, he is indeed dead; but if you worship God, He is alive and can never die."

The Holy Prophet (peace be on him) lived a full life which presents before us all possible examples of goodness as a guide for our own lives. He brough about a revolution in all areas of human conduct. The disorganized, corrupt and weak Arabs were transformed into an honorable, successful and strong people when they became Muslims and followed the injunctions of Islam in all areas of their lives.

The sacred life of the Prophet (peace be on him) examplifies the teachings of the Qur'an. He is the model of the most excellent of men for all to follow. The Prophet is neither God, nor His son, but a human being like all others who, as the Last Prophet of God, showed the way of salvation to all humanity. Qur'an testifies to this in these words:

"Certainly you have in the Messenger of God an excellent exemplar for him who hopes in God and the Last Day, and remembers God much." (33:21)

The Qur'an refers to the sanctity of the Holy Prophet (peace be on him) in these words:

"Surely God and His angels bless the Prophet. O you who believe, call for blessings on him and salute him with a worthy salutation." (33:56)

Let us pray to God to give us wisdom and strength to walk in the way of Islam according to the path shown to us by Prophet Muhammad (peace be on him), THE LAST MESSENGER OF GOD.

20. SOME SAYINGS OF PROPHET MUHAMMAD (peace be on him)

* Actions will be judged according to intentions.

* No present or gift of a parent, out of all the gifts and presents to a child, is superior to good education.

* The pleasure of God is in the pleasure of the parents and the displeasure of God is in the displeasure of the parents.

* He is not of us who is not merciful to our younger people, and does not honor the old among us.

* Seeking knowledge is an obligation for every Muslim man and woman.

* The most perfect of Muslims, in point of faith, is he who is the best among them in manners, and the best among them to his wife.

* The most hateful of all lawful things, in the sight of God, is divorce.

* By Him in Whose hand stands my life! No man believes until he loves for his brother what he loves for himself.

* He is not a true believer who eats his fill while his neighbor lies hungry by his side.

* The proof of a Muslim's sincerity is that he pays no heed to which is not his business.

* When a man dies, his works also stop, except three: acts of charity which are continued, knowledge by which all profit, and a righteous issue who prays for him.

* Verily, God is pure and loves the pure, is clean and loves the clean, is beneficent and loves the beneficent, is generous and loves the generous.

* Verily, modesty and faith are related to each other; when one of them is taken away, the other is also taken away.

* To be alone is better than to have a bad companion; and a good companion is better than being alone; and enjoining the good is better than keeping silence; and silence is better than enjoining evil.

* Forgive him who wrongs you; join him who cuts you off; do

good to him who does evil to you; and speak the truth
although it be against you.

* A man who points out the good is like one who does it.

* There are two favors (of God) which many among men are
foolish (enough) to ignore — health and leisure.

* Faith is a restraint against all violence; let no Muslim commit
violence.

* The first thing created by God was intellect.

INTRODUCTION

Meaning of the Word 'Caliph'

The word 'Caliph' is the English form of the Arabic word 'Khalifa,' which is short for *'Khalifatu Rasulil-lah'*. The latter expression means 'Successor to the Messenger of God,' the Holy Prophet Muhammad (peace be on him). The title *'Khalifatu Rasulil-lah'*. was first used for Abu Bakr, who was elected head of the Muslim community after the death of the Prophet.

The Significance of the Caliphate

The mission of Prophet Muhammad (peace be on him), like that of the earlier messengers of God, was to call people to the worship of and submission to the One True God. In practice, submission to God means to obey His injunctions as given in the Holy Qur'an and as exemplified by *Sunnah* (the practice of the Prophet). As successor to the Prophet, the Caliph was the head of the Muslim community and his primary responsibility was to continue in the path of the Prophet. Since religion was perfected and the door of Divine revelation was closed at the death of the Prophet, the Caliph was to make all laws in accordance with the Qur'an and the *Sunnah*. He was a ruler over Muslims but not their sovereign since sovereignty belongs to God alone. He was to be obeyed as long as he obeyed God. He was responsible for creating and maintaining conditions under which it would be easy for Muslims to live according to Islamic principles, and to see that justice was done to all. Abu Bakr, at the time he accepted the caliphate, stated

19

his position thus:

> "The weak among you shall be strong with me until their rights
> have been vindicated; and the strong among you shall be weak with
> me until, if the Lord wills, I have taken what is due from them ...
> Obey me as long as I obey God and His Messenger. When I dis-
> obey Him and His Prophet, then obey me not."

The Rightly-Guided Caliphs (*Al-Khulafa-ur-Rashidun*)

Those Caliphs who truly followed in the Prophet's foot-
steps are called 'The Rightly-Guided Caliphs' *(Al-Khulafa-ur-
Rashidun* in Arabic). They are the first four Caliphs: Abu
Bakr, 'Umar, Uthman and Ali. All four were among the
earliest and closest Companions of the Prophet (peace be on
him). They lived simple and righteous lives and strove hard for
the religion of God. Their justice was impartial, their treatment of others was kind and merciful, and they were one
with the people - the first among equals. After these four, the
later Caliphs assumed the manners of kings and emperors and
the true spirit of equality of ruler and ruled diminished to a
considerable extent in the political life of Muslims.

It should be clearly understood that the mission of Prophet Muhammad (peace be on him), and hence that of the
Rightly-Guided Caliphs, was *not* political, social or economic
reform, although such reforms were a logical consequence of
the success of this mission, *nor* the unity of a nation and the
establishment of an empire, although the nation did unite and
vast areas came under one administration, *nor* the spread of a
civilization or culture, although many civilizations and cultures
developed, *but only* to deliver the message of God to all the
peoples of the world and to invite them to submit to Him,
while being the foremost among those who submitted.

What About the Present?

The primary responsibility of an Islamic government is
still the same as it was in the days of the early Caliphs: to
make all laws in accordance with the Qur'an and the *Sunnah*, to
make positive efforts to create and maintain conditions under
which it will be possible and easy for Muslims to live an
Islamic life, to secure impartial and speedy justice for all, and

to strive hard in the path of God. Any government which is committed to such a policy is truly following the example of the Prophet (peace be on him).

THE FIRST CALIPH — ABU BAKR
(632-634 A.C.)

"If I were to take a friend other than my Lord, I would take Abu Bakr as a friend." (*Hadith*)

Election to the Caliphate

The Prophet's closest Companion, Abu Bakr, was not present when the Holy Prophet (peace be on him) breathed his last in the apartment of his beloved wife of later years, Aisha, Abu Bakr's daughter. When he came to know of the Prophet's passing, Abu Bakr hurried to the house of sorrow. "How blessed was your life and how beatific is your death," he whispered as he kissed the cheek of his beloved friend and master who now was no more.

When Abu Bakr came out of the Prophet's apartment and broke the news, disbelief and dismay gripped the community of Muslims in Medina. Muhammad (peace be on him) had been the leader, the guide and the bearer of Divine revelation through whom they had been brought from idolatry and barbarism into the way of God. How could he die? Even Umar, one of the bravest and strongest of the Prophet's Companions, lost his composure, drew his sword and threatened to kill anyone who said that the Prophet was dead. Abu Bakr gently pushed him aside, ascended the steps of the lectern in the mosque and addressed the people, saying

"O people, verily whoever worshipped Muhammad, behold! Muhammad is indeed dead. But whoever worships God, behold! God is alive and will never die."

And then he concluded with a verse from the Qur'an:

" ' And Muhammad is but a Messenger. Many Messengers have gone before him; if then he dies or is killed, will you turn back upon your heels?" · [3:144]

On hearing these words, the people were consoled. Despondency gave place to confidence and tranquility. This critical moment had passed. But the Muslim community was now faced with an extremely serious problem — that of choosing a leader. After some discussion among the Companions of the Prophet who had assembled in order to select a leader, it became apparent that no one was better suited for this responsibility than Abu Bakr. A portion of the speech the First Caliph gave after his election has already been quoted in the introduction.

Abu Bakr's Life

Abu Bakr ('The Owner of Camels') was not his real name. He acquired this name later in life because of his great interest in raising camels. His real name was Abdul Ka'aba ('Slave of Ka'aba'), which Muhammad (peace be on him) later changed to Abdullah ('Slave of God'). The Prophet also gave him the title of 'Siddiq' - 'The Testifier to the Truth.'

Abu Bakr was a fairly wealthy merchant, and before he embraced Islam was a respected citizen of Mecca. He was three years younger than Muhammad (peace be on him) and some natural affinity drew them together from earliest childhood. He remained the closest Companion of the Prophet all through the Prophet's life. When Muhammad first invited his closest friends and relatives to Islam, Abu Bakr was among the earliest to accept it. He also persuaded Uthman and Bilal to accept Islam. In the early days of the Prophet's mission, when the handful of Muslims were subjected to relentless persecution and torture, Abu Bakr bore his full share of hardship. Finally when God's permission came to emigrate from Mecca, he was the one chosen by the Prophet to accompany him on the dangerous journey to Medina [see Unit 2, Prophet Muhammad]. In the numerous battles which took place during the life of the Prophet, Abu Bakr was always by his side. Once he brought all his belongings to the Prophet, who was raising money for the defense of Medina. The Prophet asked, "Abu Bakr, what did you leave for your family?" The reply came: "God and His Prophet."

Even before Islam, Abu Bakr was known to be a man of upright character and. amiable and compassionate nature. All through his life he was sensitive to human suffering and kind to the poor and helpless. Even though he was wealthy, he lived very simply and spent his money for charity, for freeing slaves and for the cause of Islam. He often spent part of the night in supplication and prayer. He shared with his family a cheerful and affectionate home life.

Abu Bakr's Caliphate

Such, then, was the man upon whom the burden of leadership fell at the most sensitive period in the history of the Muslims.

As the news of the Prophet's death spread, a number of tribes rebelled and refused to pay *Zakat* (poor-due), saying that this was due only to the Prophet (peace be on him). At the same time a number of impostors claimed that the prophethood had passed to them after Muhammad, and they raised the standard of revolt. To add to all this, two powerful empires, the Eastern Roman and the Persian, also threatened the new-born Islamic state at Medina.

Under these circumstances, many Companions of the Prophet, including Umar, advised Abu Bakr to make concessions to the *Zakat* evaders, at least for a time. The new Caliph disagreed. He insisted that the Divine Law cannot be divided, that there is no distinction between the obligations of *Zakat* and *Salat* (prayer), and that any compromise with the injunctions of God would eventually erode the foundations of Islam. Umar and others were quick to realize their error of judgment. The revolting tribes attacked Medina but the Muslims were prepared. Abu Bakr himself led the charge, forcing them to retreat. He then made a relentless war on the false claimants to prophethood, most of whom submitted and again professed Islam.

The threat from the Roman Empire had actually arisen earlier, during the Prophet's lifetime. The Prophet had organized an army under the command of Usama, the son of a freed slave. The army had not gone far when the Prophet had fallen ill, so they stopped. After the death of the Prophet the question was raised whether the army should be sent again or should remain for the defense of Medina. Again Abu Bakr showed a firm determination. He said, "I shall send Usama's army on its way as ordered by the Prophet, even if I am left alone."

The final instructions he gave to Usama prescribed a code of conduct in war which remains unsurpassed to this day. Part of his instructions to the Muslim army were:

"Do not be deserters, nor be guilty of disobedience. Do not kill an old man, a woman or a child. Do not injure date palms and do not cut down fruit trees. Do not slaughter any sheep or cows or camels except for food. You will encounter persons who spend their lives in monasteries. Leave them alone and do not molest them."

Khalid bin Waleed had been chosen by the Prophet (peace be on him) on several occasions to lead Muslim armies. A man of supreme courage and a born leader, his military genius came to full flower during the Caliphate of Abu Bakr. Throughout Abu Bakr's reign Khalid led his troops from one victory to another against the attacking Romans.

Another contribution of Abu Bakr to the cause of Islam was the collection and compilation of the verses of the Qur'an.

Abu Bakr died on 21 Jamadi-al Akhir, 13 A.H. (23 August 634 A.C.), at the age of sixty-three, and was buried by the side of the Holy Prophet (peace be on him). His caliphate had been of a mere twenty-seven months duration. In this brief span, however, Abu Bakr had managed, by the Grace of God, to strengthen and consolidate his community and the state, and to secure the Muslims against the perils which had threatened their existence.

THE SECOND CALIPH – 'UMAR
(634-644 A.C.)

"God has placed truth upon Umar's tongue and heart." (*Hadith*)

'Umar's Life

During his last illness Abu Bakr had conferred with his people, particularly the more eminent among them. After this meeting they chose 'Umar as his successor.

'Umar was bórn into a respected Quraish family thirteen years after the birth of Muhammad (peace be on him). Umar's family was known for its extensive knowledge of genealogy. When he grew up, 'Umar was proficient in this branch of knowledge as well as in swordsmanship, wrestling and the art of speaking. He also learned to read and write while still a child, a very rare thing in Mecca at that time. 'Umar earned his living as a merchant. His trade took him to many foreign lands and he met all kinds of people. This experience gave him an insight into the affairs and problems of men. 'Umar's personality was dynamic, self-assertive, frank and straightforward. He always spoke whatever was in his mind even if it displeased others.

'Umar was twenty-seven when the Prophet (peace be on him) proclaimed his mission. The ideas Muhammad was preaching enraged him as much as they did the other notables of Mecca. He was just as bitter against anyone accepting Islam as others among the Quraish. When his slave-girl accepted Islam he beat her until he himself was exhausted and told her, "I have stopped because I am tired, not out of pity for you." The story of his embracing Islam is an interesting one. One day, full of anger against the Prophet, he drew his sword and set out to kill him. A friend met him on the way. When 'Umar told him what he planned to do, his friend informed him that 'Umar's own sister, Fatima, and her husband had also accepted Islam. 'Umar went straight to his sister's house where he found her reading from pages of the Qur'an. He fell upon her and beat her mercilessly. Bruised and bleeding, she told her brother, " 'Umar, you can do what you like, but you cannot turn our hearts away from Islam." These words produced a strange effect upon 'Umar. What was this faith that made even weak women so strong of heart? He asked his sister to show him what she had been reading; he was at once moved to the core by the words of the Qur'an and immediately grasped their truth. He went straight to the house where the Prophet was staying and vowed allegiance to him.

Umar made no secret of his acceptance of Islam. He gathered the Muslims and offered prayers at the Ka'aba. This boldness and devotion of an influential citizen of Mecca raised the morale of the small community of Muslims. Nonetheless 'Umar was also subjected to privations, and when permission for emigration to Medina came, he also left Mecca.

The soundness of 'Umar's judgment, his devotion to the Prophet (peace be on him), his outspokenness and uprightness won for him a trust and confidence from the Prophet which was second only to that given to Abu Bakr. The Prophet gave him the title 'Farooq,' which means the 'Separator of Truth from Falsehood." During the Caliphate of Abu Bakr, 'Umar was his closest assistant and adviser. When Abu Bakr died, all the people of Medina swore allegiance to 'Umar, and on 23 Jamadi-al-Akhir, 13 A.H., he was proclaimed Caliph.

'Umar's Caliphate

After taking charge of his office, 'Umar spoke to the Muslims of Medina:

". . . O people, you have some rights on me which you can always claim. One of your rights is that if anyone of you comes to me with a claim, he should leave satisfied. Another of your rights is that you can demand that I take nothing unjustly from the revenues of the State. You can also demand that. . . I fortify your frontiers and do not put you into danger. It is also your right that if you go to battle I should look after your families as a father would while you are away.

"O people, remain conscious of God, forgive me my faults and help me in my task. Assist me in enforcing what is good and forbidding what is evil. Advise me regarding the obligations that have been imposed upon me by God. . ."

The most notable feature of 'Umar's caliphate was the vast expansion of Islam. Apart from Arabia, Egypt. Iraq,

Palestine and Iran also came under the protection of the Islamic government. But the greatness of 'Umar himself lies in the quality of his rule. He gave a practical meaning to the Qur'anic injunction:

"O you who believe, stand out firmly for justice as witnesses to God, even as against yourselves, or your parents, or your kin, and whether it concerns rich or poor, for God can best protect both." (4:135)

Once a woman brought a claim against the Caliph 'Umar. When 'Umar appeared on trial before the judge, the judge stood up as a sign of respect toward him. 'Umar reprimanded him, saying, "This is the first act of injustice you did to this woman!"

He insisted that his appointed governors live simple lives, keep no guard at their doors and be accessible to the people at all times, and he himself set the example for them. Many times foreign envoys and messengers sent to him by his generals found him resting under a palm tree or praying in the mosque among the people, and it was difficult for them to distinguish which man was the Caliph. He spent many a watchful night going about the streets of Medina to see whether anyone needed help or assistance. The general social and moral tone of the Muslim society at that time is well-illustrated by the words of an Egyptian who was sent to spy on the Muslims during their Egyptian campaign. He reported:

"I have seen a people, every one of whom loves death more than he loves life. They cultivate humility rather than pride. None is given to material ambitions. Their mode of living is simple. . . Their commander is their equal. They make no distinction between superior and inferior, between master and slave. When the time of prayer approaches, none remains behind. . ."

'Umar gave his government an administrative structure. Departments of treasury, army and public revenues were established. Regular salaries were set up for soldiers. A population census was held. Elaborate land surveys were conducted to assess equitable taxes. New cities were founded. The areas which came under his rule were divided into provinces and governors were appointed. New roads were laid, canals were dug and wayside hotels were built. Provision was made for the support of the poor and the needy from public funds. He

28

defined, by precept and by example, the rights and privileges
of non-Muslims, an example of which is the following contract
with the Christians of Jerusalem:

> "This is the protection which the servant of God, 'Umar, the
> Ruler of the Believers, has granted to the people of Eiliya
> [Jerusalem]. The protection is for their lives and properties, their
> churches and crosses, their sick and healthy and for all their co-
> religionists. Their churches shall not be used for habitation, nor
> shall they be demolished, nor shall any injury be done to them or
> to their compounds, or to their crosses, nor shall their properties
> be injured in any way. There shall be no compulsion for these
> people in the matter of religion, nor shall any of them suffer any
> injury on account of religion. . . Whatever is written herein is
> under the covenant of God and the responsibility of His Messenger,
> of the Caliphs and of the believers, and shall hold good as long as
> they pay *Jizya* [the tax for their defense] imposed on them."

Those non-Muslims who took part in defense together with
the Muslims were _ empted from paying *Jizya*, and when the
Muslims had to retreat from a city whose non-Muslim citizens
had paid this tax for their defense, the tax was returned to the
non-Muslims. The old, the poor and the disabled of Muslims
and non-Muslims alike were provided for from the public
treasury and from the *Zakat* funds.

'Umar's Death

In 23 A.H., when 'Umar returned to Medina from *Hajj*,
he raised his hands and prayed, "O God! I am advanced in
years, my bones are weary, my powers are declining, and the
people for whom I am responsible have spread far and wide.
Summon me back to Thyself, my Lord!" Some time later,
when 'Umar went to the mosque to lead a prayer, a Magian
named Abu Lulu Feroze, who had a grudge against 'Umar on a
personal matter, attacked him with a dagger and stabbed him
several times. Umar reeled and fell to the ground. When he
learned that the assassin was a Magian, he said, "Thank
God he is not a Muslim."

'Umar died in the first week of Muharram, 24 A.H., and
was buried by the side of the Holy Prophet (peace be on him).

THE THIRD CALIPH — UTHMAN
(644-656 A.C.)

"Every Prophet has an assistant, and my assistant will be Uthman."
(*Hadith*)

Uthman's Election

When 'Umar fell under the assassin's dagger before he died
the people asked him to nominate his successor. 'Umar appointed a committee consisting of six of the ten companions
of the Prophet (peace be on him) about whom the Prophet had
said, "They are the people of Heaven" - Ali, Uthman, Abdul
Rahman, Sa'ad, Al-Zubayr and Talha - to select the next
Caliph from among themselves. He also outlined the procedure
to be followed if any differences of opinion should arise.
Abdul Rahman withdrew his name. He was then authorized
by the committee to nominate the Caliph. After two days
of discussion among the candidates and after the opinions of
the Muslims in Medina had been ascertained, the choice was
finally limited to Uthman and Ali. Abdul Rahman came to
the mosque together with other Muslims, and after a brief
speech and questioning of the two men, swore allegiance to
Uthman. All those present did the same, and Uthman became
the third Caliph of Islam in the month of Muharram, 24 A.H.

Uthman's Life

Uthman bin Affan was born seven years after the Holy
Prophet (peace be on him). He belonged to the Omayyad
branch of the Quraish tribe. He learned to read and write at
an early age, and as a young man became a successful merchant.
Even before Islam Uthman had been noted for his truthfulness
and integrity. He and Abu Bakr were close friends, and it
was Abu Bakr who brought him to Islam when he was thirty-
four years of age. Some years later he married the Prophet's
second daughter, Ruqayya. In spite of his wealth and position,
his relatives subjected him to torture because he had embraced
Islam, and he was forced to emigrate to Abyssinia. Some
time later he returned to Mecca but soon migrated to Medina
with the other Muslims. In Medina his business again began

30

to flourish and he regained his former prosperity. Uthman's generosity had no limits. On various occasions he spent a great portion of his wealth for the welfare of the Muslims, for charity and for equipping the Muslim armies. That is why he came to be known as 'Ghani,' meaning 'Generous.'

Uthman's wife, Ruqayya, was seriously ill just before the Battle of Badr, and he was excused by the Prophet (peace be on him) from participating in the battle. The illness of Ruqayya proved fatal, leaving Uthman deeply grieved. The Prophet was moved and offered Uthman the hand of another of his daughters, Kulthum. Because he had the high privilege of having two daughters of the Prophet as wives, Uthman was known as 'The Possessor of the Two Lights.'

Uthman participated in the Battles of Uhud and the Trench. After the encounter of the Trench, the Prophet (peace be on him) determined to perform *Hajj* and sent Uthman as his emissary to the Quraish in Mecca, who detained him. The episode ended in a treaty with the Meccans known as the Treaty of Hudaibiya [see Unit 2, Prophet Muhammad].

The portrait we have of Uthman is of an unassuming, honest, mild, generous and very kindly man, noted especially for his modesty and his piety. He often spent part of the night in prayer, fasted every second or third day, performed *Hajj* every year, and looked after the needy of the whole community. In spite of his wealth, he lived very simply and slept on bare sand in the courtyard of the Prophet's mosque. Uthman knew the Qur'an from memory and had an intimate knowledge of the context and circumstances relating to each verse.

Uthman's Caliphate

During Uthman's rule the characteristics of Abu Bakr's and Umar's caliphates - impartial justice' for all, mild and humane policies, striving in the path of God, and the expansion of Islam - continued. Uthman's realm extended in the west to Morocco, in the east to Afghanistan, and in the north to Armenia and Azerbaijan. During his caliphate a navy was organized, administrative divisions of the state were revised, and many public projects were expanded and completed. Uthman send prominent Companions of the Prophet (peace be on him) as his personal deputies to various provinces to scrutinize the conduct of officials and the condition of the people.

Uthman's most notable contribution to the religion of God was the compilation of a complete and authoritative text of the Qur'an. A large number of copies of this text were made and distributed all over the Muslim world.

Uthman ruled for twelve years. The first six years were marked by internal peace and tranquility, but during the second half of his caliphate a rebellion arose. The Jews and the Magians, taking advantage of dissatisfaction among the people, began conspiring against Uthman, and by publicly airing their complaints and grievances, gained so much sympathy that it became difficult to distinguish friend from foe.

It may seem surprising that a ruler of such vast territories, whose armies were matchless, was unable to deal with these rebels. If Uthman had wished, the rebellion could have been crushed at the very moment it began. But he was reluctant to be the first to shed the blood of Muslims, however rebellious they might be. He preferred to reason with them, to persuade them with kindness and generosity. He well remembered hearing the Prophet (peace be on him) say, "Once the sword is unsheathed among my followers, it will not be sheathed until the Last Day."

The rebels demanded that he abdicate and some of the Companions advised him to do so. He would gladly have followed this course of action, but again he was bound by a solemn pledge he had given to the Prophet. "Perhaps God will clothe you with a shirt, Uthman" the Prophet had told him once, "and if the people want you to take it off, do not take it off for them." Uthman said to a well-wisher on a day when his house was surrounded by the rebels, "God's Messenger made a covenant with me and I shall show endurance in adhering to it."

32

After a long siege, the rebels broke into Uthman's house and murdered him. When the first assassin's sword struck Uthman, he was reciting the verse, "Verily, God sufficeth thee: He is the All-Hearing, the All-Knowing" (2:137).

Uthman breathed his last on the afternoon of Friday, 17 Dhul Hijja, 35 A.H. (June, 656 A.C.). He was eighty-four years old. The power of the rebels was so great that Uthman's body lay unburied until Saturday night, when he was buried in his blood-stained clothes, the shroud which befits all martyrs in the cause of God.

THE FOURTH CALIPH — ALI
(656-661 A.C.)

"You [Ali] are my brother in this world and the next." (Hadith)

Ali's Election

After Uthman's martyrdom, the office of the caliphate remained unfilled for two or three days. Many people insisted that Ali should take up the office, but he was embarrassed by the fact that the people who pressed him hardest were the rebels, and he therefore declined at first. When the notable Companions of the Prophet (peace be on him) urged him, however, he finally agreed.

Ali's Life

Ali bin Abi Talib was the first cousin of the Prophet (peace be on him). More than that, he had grown up in the Prophet's own household, later married his youngest daughter, Fatima, and remained in closest association with him for nearly thirty years.

Ali was ten years old when the Divine Message came to Muhammad (peace be on him). One night he saw the Prophet and his wife Khadijah bowing and prostrating. He asked the Prophet about the meaning of their actions. The Prophet told him that they were praying to God Most High and that Ali too should accept Islam. Ali said that he would first like to ask his father about it. He spent a sleepless night, and in the morning he went to the Prophet and said, "When God created me, He did not consult my father, so why should I consult my father in order to serve God?" and he accepted the truth of Muhammad's message.

When the Divine command came, "And warn thy nearest relatives" (26:214), Muhammad (peace be on him) invited his relatives for a meal. After it was finished, he addressed them and asked, "Who will join me in the cause of God?" There was utter silence for a while, and then Ali stood up. "I am the youngest of all present here," he said. "My eyes trouble me because they are sore and my legs are thin and weak, but I shall join you and help you in whatever way I can." The

34

assembly broke up in derisive laughter. But during the difficult wars in Mecca, Ali stood by these words and faced all the hardships to which the Muslims were subjected. He slept in the bed of the Prophet when the Quraish planned to murder Muhammad. It was he to whom the Prophet entrusted, when he left Mecca, the valuables which had been given to him for safekeeping, to be returned to their owners [see Unit 2, Prophet Muhammad].

Apart from the expedition of Tabuk, Ali fought in all the early battles of Islam with great distinction, particularly in the expedition of Khaybar. It is said that in the Battle of Uhud he recieved more than sixteen wounds.

The Prophet (peace be on him) loved Ali dearly and called him by many fond names. Once the Prophet found him sleeping in the dust. He brushed off Ali's clothes and said fondly, "Wake up, Abu Turab (Father of Dust)." The Prophet also gave him the title of 'Asadullah' ('Lion of God').

Ali's humility, austerity, piety, deep knowledge of the Qur'an and his sagacity gave him great distinction among the Prophet's Companions. Abu Bakr, 'Umar and Uthman consulted him frequently during their caliphates. Many times 'Umar had made him his vice-regent at Medina when he was away. Ali was also a great scholar of Arabic literature and pioneered in the field of grammar and rhetoric. His speeches, sermons and letters served for generations afterward as models of literary expression. Many of his wise and epigrammatic sayings have been preserved. Ali thus had a rich and versatile personality. In spite of these attainments he remained a modest and humble man. Once during his caliphate when he was going about the marketplace, a man stood up in respect and followed him. "Do not do it," said Ali. "Such manners are a temptation for a ruler and a disgrace for the ruled."

Ali and his household lived extremely simple and austere lives. Sometimes they even went hungry themselves because of Ali's great generosity, and none who asked for help was ever turned away from his door. His plain, austere style of living did not change even when he was ruler over a vast domain.

Ali's Caliphate

As mentioned previously, Ali accepted the caliphate very reluctantly. Uthman's murder and the events surrounding it were a symptom, and also became a cause, of civil strife on a large scale. Ali felt that the tragic situation was mainly due to inept governors. He therefore dismissed all the governors who had been appointed by Uthman and appointed new ones. All the governors excepting Muawiya, the governor of Syria, submitted to his orders. Muawiya declined to obey until Uthman's blood was avenged. The Prophet's widow Aisha also took the position that Ali should first bring the murderers to trial. Due to the chaotic conditions during the last days of Uthman it was very difficult to establish the identity of the murderers, and Ali refused to punish anyone whose guilt was not lawfully proved. Thus a battle between the army of Ali and the supporters of Aisha took place. Aisha later realized her error of judgment and never forgave herself for it.

The situation in Hijaz (the part of Arabia in which Mecca and Medina are located) became so troubled that Ali moved his capital to Iraq. Muawiya now openly rebelled against Ali and a fierce battle was fought between their armies. This battle was inconclusive, and Ali had to accept the *de facto* government of Muawiya in Syria.

However, even though the era of Ali's caliphate was marred by civil strife, he nevertheless introduced a number of reforms, particularly in the levying and collecting of revenues.

It was the fortieth year of *Hijra*. A fanatical group called Kharijites, consisting of people who had broken away from Ali due to his compromise with Muawiya, claimed that neither Ali, the Caliph, nor Muawiya, the ruler of Syria, nor Amr bin al-Aas, the ruler of Egypt, were worthy of rule. In fact, they went so far as to say that the true caliphate came to an end with 'Umar and that Muslims should live without any ruler over them except God. They vowed to kill all three rulers, and assassins were dispatched in three directions.

The assassins who were deputed to kill Muawiya and Amr did not succeed and were captured and executed, but Ibn-e-Muljim, the assassin who was commissioned to kill Ali, accomplished his task. One morning when Ali was absorbed in prayer in a mosque, Ibn-e-Muljim stabbed him with a poisoned sword. On the 20th of Ramadan, 40 A.H., died the last of the Rightly-Guided Caliphs of Islam. May God Most High be pleased with them and grant to them His eternal reward.

6. CONCLUSION

With the death of Ali, the first and most notable phase in the history of Muslim peoples came to an end. All through this period it had been the Book of God and the practices of His Messenger—that is, the Qur'an and the *Sunnah*—which had guided the leaders and the led, set the standards of their moral conduct and inspired their actions. It was the time when the ruler and the ruled, the rich and the poor, the powerful and the weak, were uniformly subject to the Divine Law. It was an epoch of freedom and equality, of God-consciousness and humility, of social justice which recognized no privileges, and of an impartial law which accepted no pressure groups or vested interests.

After Ali, Muawiya assumed the caliphate and thereafter the caliphate became hereditary, passing from one king to another.

1. INTRODUCTION

The Meaning of the Words 'Messenger' and 'Prophet'

The Arabic world *'rasul'* means 'one who is sent' or 'a messenger', and the word *'nabi'* means 'one who carries information or proclaims news'. We shall render these words as 'messenger' and 'prophet' respectively. In the religious sense, both words signify a man chosen by God to deliver His message, given to him by means of Divine revelation, to a people or, in the case of Prophet Muhammad (peace be on him), to all mankind. There is no implication of 'prophecy' or knowledge of future events in the word 'prophet' as used in the Islamic sense.

Some of the Prophets Mentioned in Qur'an

From the Qur'anic verse,

"For We assuredly send amongst every people a messenger (with the command), 'Serve God and avoid evil...' " (16:36)

we know that there have been a great number of prophets in the world. Only some among them are mentioned in Qur'an, for it is stated,

"And there are messengers who We have mentioned to thee before this and (other) messengers who We have not mentioned to thee."

(4:164)

Among those who are named in Qur'an are the following:

Adam	Nuh (Noah)
Saleh	Shu'aib
Hud	Ibrahim (Abraham
Lut (Lot)	Isma'il (Ishmael)
Ishaq (Isaac)	Y'aqub (Jacob)
Yusuf (Joseph)	Yunus (Jonah)
Musa (Moses)	Harun (Aaron)
Ayyub (Job)	Daud (David)

Sulaiman (Solomon)   Ilyas (Elijah)
Al-Yas'a (Elisha)   Dhul-Kifl (Ezekiel)
Idrees   Zakariah (Zachariah)
Yahya (John the Baptist)
'Isa (Jesus)   Muhammad (peace and the blessings
                        of God be on them all).

From Qur'an and *Hadith* (sayings of Prophet Muhammad) we also know that Muhammad (peace be on him) was the last prophet and messenger of God.

The Nature of Divine Revelation

From Qur'an and sound *Hadiths* we know that the Divine revelation came to the prophets of God through the agency of angels—spiritual beings who carry out God's commands—who appeared to them in human or angelic form and communicated the messages of God in direct speech. The only exception was in the case of Moses (peace be on him), to whom God spoke directly (4:164). In this unit the words 'Divine revelation' are used exclusively to denote this way of communication from God to His prophets.

The knowledge of the Unseen — concerning the attributes of God, the coming of the Day of Judgment and the Life after Death — which has come to us through the prophets by means of Divine revelation has the certainty of truth. On the other hand, the theories of philosophers, however plausible they may seem, are purely speculative and lack this certainty, as they stem from the limited understanding of the human mind. For the same reason, the prophetic knowledge is different in character and beyond comparison with the knowledge claimed to have been obtained through 'intuition,' 'inspiration,' 'mystical experience' and 'spiritual enlightenment' by poets, mystics, seers and saints.

The Characteristics of Prophets

1. The prophets of God were human beings. Many people have found this hard to accept and have gone astray because of their inability to grasp this simple fact.

"What kept men back from believing, when guidance came to them, was nothing but this: they said, 'Has God sent a man (like us) to be (His) messenger?' " (17:94)

39

One can fall into error in this respect in either of two ways: either by refusing to believe in the prophets and their message, considering them to be impostors, or by glorifying them to the extent of considering them super-human beings or 'incarnations of God.'

2. The prophets of God were true to their trust and were examples of moral conduct, although, like any other human being, capable of errors of judgment and human weaknesses. They obeyed God's injunctions and exemplified what they taught. Qur'an says:

"No prophet can be false to his trust." (3:161)

More specifically, with reference to particular prophets,

"Surely Abraham was a model, obedient to God, by nature upright, and he was not of the polytheists." (16:120)

"And We admitted him [Lot] to Our mercy, for he was one of the righteous." (21:75)

"And Ishmael, Idrees, Ezekiel, all men of patience. We admitted them to Our mercy, for they were of the righteous ones."
(21:85-86)

3. Some of the prophets performed extraordinary acts, which we call 'miracles', by God's permission. Although a miracle in itself is not a proof of the truth of a message, on occasion it served to demonstrate the truthfulness of the messengers of God.

The Role of Prophets in History

The continued appearance of the prophets during various times and among different nations in the past is an indication of the continuity of Divine guidance and of the active interest of of God in man's destiny, both in this world and in the Hereafter. Qur'an tells us that although man's physical and biological origin is earthly — "We made you out of dust, then out of sperm" (22:5) — the main purpose of his creation is to worship God (51:56).

The concept of worship set forth in Qur'an is very broad and includes all aspects of man's life, personal and interpersonal. True worship is to love God and to have complete faith and trust in Him as a child has in his parents, to obey His injunctions, to strive for establishing His laws of social justice, kindness and co-operation among men, to oppose the tyranny and lordship of one man over another, and to call people to accept the guidance from God. Islam is the name given by Qur'an to this way of life. This way is not merely a set of beliefs and acts of piety, but requires a continual striving to attain the highest moral and spiritual values, not only in personal but also in inter-personal, economic, social, political and international affairs.

Qur'an tells us that Islam is the religion — the way of life — ordained for man by God (5:4). This means that it began not with Prophet Muhammad (peace be on him), but by the time the first man had appeared on earth.

When God created the universe, He provided everything with a 'nature' and guided it accordingly (20:50). The physical world has no choice but to obey God's guidance, which we understand as 'natural laws'. As Qur'an says:

"...It is unto Him that whatever is in the heavens and on earth surrenders itself, willingly or unwillingly, since unto Him all must return." (3:83)

For man too there is a nature, spiritual as well as physical. As far as his body is concerned, it is a part of the physical and biological world. In the spiritual and moral sphere, similarly, there is a natural way — a straight way — ordained for man by God. However, in this aspect of his life, he has been given a choice (13:31), and this distinguishes him from the rest of creation. With this freedom of choice there is a great responsibility. Since the consequences of failing in God's trust go beyond the present life and extend into the Life after Death, the challenge to man seems enormous.

As a part of his nature, God equipped man with a well-proportioned body (95:4), excellent intellectual capacities (2:31), and power to control earthly resources (22:65). He implanted into man's soul the belief in God (7:172) and endowed him with a love of knowledge, truth and beauty — a breathing of God's spirit into man which made him superior to the angels (38:71-72). Finally, to provide man with firm guidance to enable him to make the right choices with the

41

degree of freedom which God gave him, He raised messengers among men who brough His revelation concerning the right way to live and warned of the consequences of deviating from it.

From Noah to Muhammad (peace be on them), all the prophets proclaimed this same message of Islam, originating not in their own minds but with God. Every prophet not only proclaimed the truth of God's Oneness and called people to submit to Him, but also set an example with their own lives and strove hard to establish the Divinely-ordained laws of moral conduct, social justice, brotherhood and co-operation among men. The humble, the poor, the oppressed, the seekers after truth, and upright were the first to follow the prophets, while the proud, the powerful, the rich, the pleasure-lowing and those who blindly accepted current beliefs and practices opposed them (7:59-93).

Among the numerous prophets of God were Abraham, Moses and Jesus (peace be on them). Abraham's achievement was the effective proclamation of the Oneness of God. Never since his time has mankind entirely forgotten that it is God alone Who deserves our worship, our devotion and our most fervent love. Moses' followers preserved a part of the message he brought, but they added to it many cumbersome details, reducing the Divine law to mere ritual and so thoroughly confusing God's guidance with the additions of man that it became impossible to distinguish between them. They also came to believe that God's guidance was limited only to themselves. The followers of Jesus understood that the message was universal, but, by elevating Jesus to the status of God, compromised the central truth of his message — the Unity and Sublimity of God.

Finally, in the clear light of recorded history, God in His great mercy sent His last messenger, Muhammad (peace be on him). For all time to come, a final, clear and complete statement of God's guidance — the Qur'an — was given to mankind. A messenger was appointed from among men who delivered this guidance, interpreted it, and exemplified it in his life. A community was organized which preserved the message faithfully, acted upon it, and carried it throughout the world.

"You [the Muslims] are indeed the best community which has ever been brought forth for (the good of) mankind; you enjoin the doing of what is right and forbid the doing of what is wrong, and you believe in God." (3:110)

The truth had been declared before, but it had remained an unattained ideal. But this time it became a concrete reality — a people living according to the Divine standards of brotherhood, kindness, social justice, moral integrity and personal piety, who strove with their lives and possessions so that "the word of God remained supreme" (9:40).

Thus Islam, the Divinely-ordained way of life for man, began its full career in human history in the time of Prophet Muhammad (peace be on him) in the Seventh Century after Jesus.

God's guidance to man has been completed in Qur'an, and the last prophet of God has come and gone. Yet the struggle continues between those who strive so that the word of God may *remain* supreme and those who, considering themselves unaccountable to God, cling to man-made theories, laws and practices.

In order to increase understanding of the mission of the prophets, this unit presents the lives and teachings of three prophets who have left a great impact on the history of mankind: Abraham, Moses and Jesus (peace and God's blessings be on them). The accounts in this unit are based on Qur'anic narrative, which emphasizes those aspects of the lives of the prophets which have moral and spiritual significance. The reader will notice that many events in the life of earlier prophets were similar in circumstances to events in the life of Prophet Muhammad (peace be on him). Knowledge of what had happened to other messengers of God brought comfort and strength to the Prophet and his Companions in facing persecution and wars of aggression.

43

2. ABRAHAM (IBRAHIM)

"Who could be better in religion than one who submits his whole self to God, does good, and follows the way of Abraham, the true in faith? For God took Abraham for a friend." (4:125)

The events in the life of Abraham (peace be on him) are described in Qur'an in many places, among which are the following verses: 2:124-135, 6:74-83, 11:69-76, 14:35-41, 15:51-60, 19:41-50, 21:51-71, 26:70-87, 29:16-25, 37:83-111 and 51:24-37.

Early Life

Abraham (peace be on him), the son of Azar, was born in the city of Ur in the land of the Chaldeans (Iraq) roughly 4,000 years ago.   The guidance which God had given through the earlier prophets had been forgotten and people worshipped idols.   Among such people Abraham was brought up and was chosen by God to be His messenger.

Even as a young man, he began talking to his father, his family and other people concerning the erroneousness and futility of worshipping idols or the heavenly bodies. He argued with them, appealing to their intellect and reason. Their only answer to him was: "We found our fathers worshipping these statues."   Qur'an 21:51-70 relates how, in their absence, Abraham broke to pieces their idols, excepting the biggest one. When they returned and questioned him, he replied: "Ask the idols if they can speak!" At this, they realized with shame that the worshipping of idols was senseless. But, as is usual with people who are so committed to their way of life that they would rather suppress the truth than acknowledge their error and change their ways, their only reaction was: "Burn Abraham and protect your gods!" But God delivered His messenger from the fire: "We said, 'O fire! Be cool and safe for Abraham.'" (21:69).

Ishmael (Isma'il)

Later in his life Abraham (peace be on him), at God's command, left his country for another land — Canaan (Palestine). In his company were his wife Sarah, his nephew the Prophet Lot (Lut) and his servants. Years later they came back to Negeb, from where Lot (peace be on him) migrated to Sodom. Abraham was old and he had no children so at his wife's suggestion, he took her personal servant, Hagar (Hajira), as wife. In response to his prayers, God granted him a son by Hagar whom he named Ishmael (Isma'il). A little later God commanded him to take Hagar and the baby boy to a place in Arabia and leave them there. He brought them to a valley called Batha and left them at the place where the city of Mecca later grew. The valley was dry and without any vegatation. Soon Hagar and her son ran out of water, and Ishmael began to cry with thirst. The mother ran between the surrounding hills to look for water, crying and beseeching God for help. When she finally returned to the baby, she found a spring of water coming out of the ground where he had dug his heels. The water of this spring, called the Well of Zamzam, gushes forth to this day. The observance of *Sa'ai* (Hastening) (see Unit 5b: Pilgrimage) is a part of the *Hajj* observances in commemoration of Hagar's running between the two hills, Safa and Marwa.

The Ordeal of Sacrifice

Soon many tribes of Arabia came to settle in the valley of Batha and shared their life with Abraham's family. Abraham (peace be on him) visited them a number of times. When Ishmael was a young man, Abraham dreamed that he had sacrificed his only son, Ishmael (Isaac was not yet born), to God. This dream recurred on three successive nights. Interpreting it to be a command from God, Abraham told it to his son and asked his opinion concerning it. Ishmael was ready at once to obey and to submit. However, it was but a test of Abraham's faith and his willingness to submit to God, and a ram was substituted for sacrifice. In this way, for all time to come, God made it clear that human sacrifice, which was practiced in antiquity by idol-worshippers, was prohibited.

In commemoration of Abraham's and Ishmael's total submission to God, Muslims all over the world celebrate Eid-ul-Adha (see Unit 10: Muslim Holidays and Ceremonies) by sacrificing a lamb, a cow or a camel and sharing its meat with friends, relatives and with the poor and needy.

The Building of Ka'aba

With Ishmael, Abraham (peace be on them) built Ka'aba, the first structure ever erected for the worship of God, in the valley of Mecca.

"And when Abraham and Ishmael were raising the foundations of the House (they prayed): 'O our Sustainer! Accept Thou this from us, for, verily, Thou alone art All-Hearing, All-Knowing! O our Sustainer! Make us surrender ourselves unto Thee, and make out of our offspring a community that shall surrender itself unto Thee, and show us our ways of worship, and accept our repentance, for, verily, Thou alone art the Acceptor of repentance, the Dispenser of grace.' " (2:127-128)

The Birth of Isaac (Ishaq)

After these events, Abraham (peace be on him) received the good news from God of the coming of another son by Sarah, his wife, to be named Isaac (Ishaq). Sarah was amazed at this and exclaimed, "How shall I bear a son when I am a very old woman and this my husband is a very old man? Surely this is a strange thing!" Yet God creates what He pleases, and thus Sarah bore Abraham a son at a very advanced age.

The Old Testament book of Genesis states that Abraham (peace be on him) died at the age of one hundred and seventy-five years. In all his ways he was an example for all time to come of an upright man whose devotion to His God came before all other loyalties.

Abraham's Character

Qur'an testifies to Abraham's devotion to God, his high moral character and purity of faith in many places. Thus we read:

"Abraham was indeed a model, devoutly obedient to God, true in faith, and he did not join gods with God. He showed his gratitude for the favors of God, Who chose him and guided him to a straight way. And We gave him good in this world, and he will be, in the Hereafter, in the ranks of the righteous." (16:120-122)

"Abraham was forbearing, tender-hearted and oft-returning to God." (11:75)

"He [Abraham] came to His Sustainer with a sound heart." (38:84)

"And who, unless he be given to folly, would want to abandon Abraham's creed, seeing that We have indeed raised him high in this world and that, verily, in the life to come he shall be among the righteous? When his Sustainer said to him, 'Submit,' he said, 'I submit to the Sustainer of the worlds.' " (2:130-131)

Abraham's Teachings

Even before his prophethood, Abraham (peace be on him) used to wonder about the objects of man's worship, which included, besides idols, the sun, moon and stars. From the beginning he rejected idols, and after along period of meditation his sound mind came to the conclusion that one should worship and obey only one's Creator. But Who is the Creator and Sustainer of all thing? In Qur'an his quest for the deepest truth, the Unity of God, is described thus:

"And, lo, (thus) spoke Abraham to his father Azar: 'Do you take idols for gods? Certainly, I see that you and your people have gone astray.' And thus We showed Abraham (God's) dominion over the heavens and the earth, that he might be of those having sure faith. When the night overshadowed him, he saw a star and said: 'This is my Sustainer!' But when it went down, he said: 'I love not the things which go down.' Then, when he saw the moon rising, he said: 'This is my Sustainer!' But when it went down, he said: 'Indeed, if my Sustainer does not guide me, I will most certainly become one of the people who go astray!' Then, when saw the sun rising, he said: 'This is my Sustainer! This is the greatest (of all)!' But when it (too) went down, he said: 'O my people ! Surely I am clear of that which you associate with God. I have turned my face to Him Who originated the heavens and the earth, a man of pure faith; for I am not of those who ascribe divinity to anything besides Him.' " (6:74-79)

Soon God appoirted him a messenger to his people. Abraham (peace be on him), who had been so dauntless even before his messengership, now reasoned and argued with great vigor with his father and his people about the senselessness of idolatry, inviting them to submit to the One True God, Who has no equals and no associates, and to become a God-conscious and a moral people.

"We bestowed aforetime on Abraham his rectitude of conduct, and We were well-acquainted with him. Behold, he said to his father and his people: 'What are these images to which you are so devoted?' They replied: 'We found our fathers worshipping them.' He said: 'Indeed, you and your fathers have been in manifest error.' They said: 'Have you come with sincerity and truth or merely jesting?' He said: 'Nay, your Sustainer is the Sustainer of the heavens and earth, Who created them; and I am a witness to this (truth).' " (21:51-56)

"And (We sent) Abraham. He said to his people: 'Worship God and be conscious of Him; that is best for you if you understand. For you worship idols besides God, and you invent falsehood. The things you worship besides God have no power to provide you sustenance. Then seek your sustenance from God, worship Him, and be grateful to Him; to Him will you return. And if you reject (the truth), so did generations before you; the duty of the messenger is only to deliver the message publicly.' " (29:16-18)

"Art thou not aware of him who argued with Abraham about his Sustainer, because God had granted him power? Abraham said: 'My Sustainer is He Who gives life and causes death.' He replied: 'I (too) give life and cause death!' Said Abraham: 'Verily, God causes the sun to rise in the east; cause it, then, to rise from the west!' Then he who was bent on denying the truth remained dumfounded; for God does not guide those who (deliberately) do wrong." (2:258)

And this is the legacy which Abraham (peace be on him) left to his sons, which has come to us, as Muslims, to this day:

" 'O my children! Behold, God has granted you the purest faith; so do not allow death to overtake you unless you be Muslims [that is, those who submit to God].' " (2:132)

References

[1] *The Old Testament:* Genesis.

[2] Ali Musa Raza Muhajir, *Lessons from the Stories of the Quran*, Sheikh Muhammad Ashraf, Lahore, 1965.

3. MOSES (MUSA)

"And to Moses God spoke directly." (4:164)

The events in the life of Moses (peace be on him) are described in Qur'an in many places, primarily in the following verses: 7:103-156, 10:75-92, 18:60-82, 20:9-98, 26:10-69, 28:4-35, 40:23-46 and 43:46-56.

Historical Background

Some four hundred years had elapsed since Joseph (the great-grandson of Abraham, and a prophet), his parents, brothers and their families had settled in Egypt. Their descendants, the Israelites (from Israel, or Jacob, Joseph's father, who was also a prophet) increased in number. These were divided into twelve tribes according to their descent from the twelve sons of Jacob (peace be on him).

The king (Pharaoh) of Egypt, possibly Ramses II (1300-1234 B.C.) was a tyrant, and he and his ruling council and priests were cruel and oppressive to the common people, especially to the Israelites. Pharaoh and his advisers, fearing that at some point the Israelites might revolt, reduced them to the status of slaves and employed them in hard labor, increasing the burden of work upon them to more than they could fulfill. Finally, fearing the increase of their numbers, Pharaoh ordered his men to throw the male babies born to the Israelites into the River Nile.

The Early Life of Moses

These were the conditions in Egypt when Moses (peace be on him) was born. Through the guidance of God, his mother kept him in secrecy for a few months and then, when she became afraid for his safety, she put him into a reed basket and set it afloat on the Nile. She stationed her daughter Miriam nearby to see what would happen to the baby. A little further down the river, Pharaoh's wife happened to see the basket and had it taken out of the water. Seeing a handsome baby boy in it, she took him to the palace and pre-

49

vailed on Pharaoh not only to spare his life but also to adopt
him as a son. It then became necessary to find a woman to
nurse him. Moses' sister Miriam came forward and, in the
words of Qur'an, said:

> "Shall I point out to you the people of a house who will nourish
> and bring him up for you and be sincerely attached to him?'
> Thus did We restore him to his mother. . ." (28:12-13)

Thus, through the guidance of God, Moses, through whose agency Pharaoh was eventually overthrown, was brought up in
his household as his own son.

Although Moses (peace be on him) grew up as part of
Pharaoh's family, one can imagine what a great sympathy for
his own people he acquired from his mother. One day while
he was walking through the streets, he saw an Egyptian and
an Israelite fighting. The Israelite called to him for help.
Moses gave a blow to the Egyptian which accidentally proved
to be fatal. In great distress, Moses cried to God for forgiveness and help:

> "He prayed, 'O my Sustainer! I have indeed wronged myself.
> Do Thou forgive me!' So (God) forgave him, for He is the Oft-
> Forgiving and the Most Merciful." (28:16)

The next day Moses (peace be on him) found out that
the news of what he had done had spread and that he was
being hunted to be killed in retaliation. He fled and went to
Madyan in western Arabia. He was resting near a watering
place for sheep when he saw two girls waiting at a distance
with their flocks. He made way for them among the rough
shepherds and gave water to their sheep. Afterwards he went
back into the shade and prayed:

> " 'O my Sustainer! Surely I am in need of whatever good Thou
> mayest send down to me.' " (28:24)

After some time, one of the girls came back to him and
very shyly asked him to come with her to her father's house.
Moses (peace be on him) went with her and told his story
to her father, who sympathized with him. At the suggestion
of the girl, he offered Moses employment and also the hand of
one of his daughters on the condition that Moses would work
for him for at least eight years. Moses gladly accepted both
offers.

Call to Messengership

After fulfilling his term of employment, Moses (peace be on him) set out for another place with his family. On the way, he saw a fire in the direction of a mountain.

"He said to his family: Wait here. I see a fire; maybe I will bring you from there some information or a burning firebrand so that you may warm yourselves.' But when he came to it, a voice was heard from the right bank of the valley, from a tree in blessed ground: 'O Moses! Verily I am God, the Sustainer of the Worlds. Throw down thy staff.' But when he saw it moving (of its own accord) as if it had been a snake, he turned back in retreat and did not retrace his steps. (God said): 'O Moses! Draw near and do not be afraid, for surely thou art in security. Insert thy hand into thy bosom, and it will come forth white without blemist; and draw thy hand close to thy side (to guard) against fear. So these shall be two signs from thy Sustainer to Pharaoh and his council, for surely they are a wicked people.' " (28:29-33)

God then communicated to Moses (peace be on him) the nature of his mission. He was to go to Pharaoh and ask him to submit to the Lord of the universe and to release the Israelites from slavery. Moses asked God to appoint his brother Aaron (Harun, also a prophet) as his helper, as Aaron was more eloquent (there are some traditions to the effect that Moses had a speech defect from childhood, when he had burned his tongue on a glowing coal). God granted Moses his request and said:

" 'Go, therefore, thou and thy brother, with My signs, and do not neglect to remember Me. Go to Pharaoh, for he has become insolent; yet speak to him gently, that he may perhaps be mindful or may fear. . .and say: 'We are messengers of thy Sustainer, so send forth with us the Children of Israel and do not oppress them. We have brought thee a sign from thy Sustainer; and peace be upon him who follows the guidance.' ' " (20:42-44,47)

Thus they went to Pharaoh.

"Pharaoh said: 'Who is thy Sustainer, Moses?' He said: 'Our Sustainer is He Who created everything, then guided it. . .He Who made for you the earth like a carpet spread out. . .and has sent down water from tne sky.' " (20:49-50,53)

In this manner, Moses (peace be on him) first brought to Pharaoh the message of the Oneness of God before requesting him to release the Israelites from slavery. However Pharaoh threatened to imprison him if he took any god besides Pharaoh himself. God then sent a series of signs in the form of various disasters which severly afflicted Pharaoh and all his people, and finally Pharaoh permitted the Israelites to depart from Egypt under the leadership of Moses.

"And We revealed to Moses: 'Travel by night with My servants, and strike (with thy rod) a dry path for them through the sea, without fear of being overtaken (by Pharaoh) and without (any other) fear.' Pharaoh followed them with his armies, but they were overwhelmed by the sea. So Pharaoh had led his people astray and was no guide to them." (20:77-79)

Life in the Wilderness

References to the life in the wilderness are contained in many places in Qur'an, especially in 2:51-83, 7:138-162 and 20:86-98.

With guidance from God, Moses (peace be on him) led his people into the wilderness of Sinai. The journey was difficult. Water was scare, food was lacking and existence was precarious. It was a time of murmuring, discontent, internal strife, rebellion against Moses, and above all, lack of faith. When Moses went up to the mountain, where God revealed to him the Law, staying for forty days, the Israelites slipped back into the idolatry to which they had grown accustomed in Egypt. They fabricated a calf from their golden ornaments and worshipped it, in spite of the protestations of Aaron, Moses' brother who was their leader during his absence. However, God's help came to them in the form of water and food - sap of plants (*mun* or manna) and flocks of quails (*salwa*) - and His guidance in the form of a moral law (the Covenant) by which they were to live.

"O Children of Israel! Remember those blessings of Mine with which I have graced you, and how I preferred you above all other people ... And when We saved you from Pharaoh's people, who afflicted you with cruel suffering. . .and when We appointed for Moses forty nights [on Mount Sinai], and in his absence you took to worshipping the (golden) calf, and thus you became wrong-doers; yet, even after that, We blotted out this your sin, so that you might be grateful. And we gave Moses the Scripture and the Criterion [to distinguish between right and wrong] so that you

might be guided. . .and We caused the clouds to comfort you
with their shade, and sent down unto you manna and quails,
(saying): 'Eat of the good things which We have provided for you as
sustenance'. . .And when Moses prayed for water for his people,
and We replied: 'Strike the rock with your staff!' - whereupon
twelve springs gushed forth from it... And when you said: 'O
Moses, indeed, we cannot endure only one kind of food; pray, then,
to thy Sustainer that He bring forth for us something of what
grows from the earth - of its herbs, its cucumbers, its garlic, its
onions.' Said (Moses): 'Would you take a lesser thing in exchange
for what is better? Go back in shame to Egypt, and then you can
have what you are asking for!' " (2:47-51)

In this fashion, over a period of forty years, the indomit-
able Moses (peace be on him), through the guidance and the
help of God, blended a motley crowd of ex-slaves into a God-
fearing nation. The first generation of people - the adults who
came with Moses from Egypt - remained to the end vacillating
and cowardly, and God denied them entrance into the land
which he had promised to them.

"And lo, Moses said unto his people: 'O my people! Remember
the blessings which God bestowed upon you . . .Enter the sacred
land which God has promised you; but do not turn back, for then
you will be lost.' They answered: 'O Moses! Behold, ferocious
people live there; never shall we enter it until they leave it. If
(once) they leave, then we shall enter.' (Whereupon) two men
from among those who feared (God, and) whom God had blessed
said: 'Enter upon them through the gate - for as soon as you enter
it, surely you shall be victorious! And in God you must place
your trust if you are believers!' They said: 'O Moses! Never shall
we enter that (land) so long as those others are in it. Go forth,
then, thou and thy Sustainer, and fight, the two of you! We shall
remain here.' He said: 'O my Sustainer! Over none do I have
power except myself and my brother; draw Thou, then, a dividing
line between us and these rebellious people.' God said: 'Then,
verily, this (land) shall be forbidden to them for forty years, while
they wander on earth, bewildered, to and fro; and do not grieve
over these rebellious people.' " (5:22-29)

Moses (peace be on him) had now grown old, and his
task was finished. According to the Old Testament book of
Exodus, he died at the age of one hundred and twenty years.
After his death, the Israelites at last entered Palestine.

The Problem of the Torah (Pentateuch)

Among the thirty-nine books of Jewish canonical scripture (the 'Old Testament' part of the Bible), the first five books - Genesis, Exodus, Leviticus, Numbers and Deuteronomy - are called the Torah ('The Teaching') by the Jews. These five books are also referred to as the Pentateuch ('Five Scrolls') and as the Books of Moses. However, Moses did not write these books and the Divine revelation to Moses, referred to in Qur'an as *Taurat*, is not identical with the Jewish Torah. (It may also be mentioned that the Divine revelation to David, referred to in Qur'an as *Zabur*, is also not identical with the Psalms of David in the Old Testament.)

The Qur'an states:

> "Then woe to those who write the books with their own hands, and then say, 'This is from God,' in order to acquire a trifling gain thereby." (2:79)

This statement is made in regard to the Jewish scripture. For many centuries Jews and Christians alike vehemently denied any addition or interpolation in their scriptures. However, over the past two hundred years a tremendous amount of research has been done by Biblical scholars on the authorship and authenticity of both the Jewish and Christian scriptures. The following statement is a summary of the views of modern Biblical scholars concerning the Torah (see reference [2] and [3]):

"Among Biblical scholars, the dominant view is that the Pentateuch [i.e., the Jewish Torah, consisting of the first five books of the Old Testament, commonly ascribed to Moses] is a composite work in which several literary sources have been blended together. According to this hypothesis, which rests on the critical labors of more than two centuries of intensive study, there are four main literary strands. . . These strands were woven together in various stages until the Pentateuch assumed its final form in about 400 B.C." (reference [2], pp. 12-13).

What, then, was God's revelation to Moses (peace be on him) and His covenant with the Israelites? In Qur'an we find passages in which these are described:

> "And lo! We accepted this solemn covenant [pledge] from the Children of Israel: You shall worship none but God, and shall

do good to your parents and relatives and orphans and the poor,
and you shall speak to all people in a goodly way, and you shall
be constant in prayer and practice regular charity ... And lo! We
accepted your solemn pledge that you would not shed one another's
blood, and would not drive one another from your homelands."
(2:83-84)

"And We ordained for them in that (*Taurat*): A life for a life, an
eye for an eye, and a nose for a nose, and an ear for an ear, and
a tooth for a tooth, and a (similar) retaliation for wounds [that
is, punishment justly proportionate to the crime committed, rather
than punishment out of all proportion to the crime, or revenge];
but he who shall forgo it out of charity will atone thereby for
some of his past sins." (5:48)

Comparing the Ten Commandments as we know them
today with the Qur'anic passages quoted above, one may con-
clude that these were part of the Divine revelation given to
Moses (peace be on him) but not probably in the present expanded form.

Through God's revelation to Moses (peace be on him) andl
the leadership which this prophet exercised, by virtue of the
insight which God had given him, over the Israelites, something
like a community dedicated to upholding the laws of God was
formed. But gradually the Divine laws were forgotten, changed
or ignored. Gradually the community which God had guided
for the most part forgot what God had given them. Nevertheless, what remained of the Divine guidance served as a preparation for the guidance which was to come through the
later prophets, particularly through Jesus and Muhammad
(peace be on them), and set the stage for later advances of
mankind toward the straight path of Islam which God had
ordained for them.

References

[1] *The Old Testament*: Exodus, Leviticus, Numbers and
    Deuteronomy.
[2] B. W. Anderson, *Understanding the Old Testament*,
    Prentice-Hall, Inc., 1957.
[3] A. S. Peake, *A Commentary on the Bible*, Thomas Nelson
    & Sons, 1952 Edition.

4. JESUS ('ISA)

"A sign unto men and a mercy from Us." (19:21)

References to Jesus (peace be on him) are contained in the following verses of Qur'an: 3:35-59, 4:157-159, 5:19, 49, 75, 78, 113-121, 6:85, 9:30, 19:1-35, 23:50, 43:57-64, 57:27 and 61:6, 14.

Historical Background

In 63 B.C. Palestine was conquered by Rome. The Roman Empire of that time did not interfere much in the affairs of its subject peoples as long as its interests were not challenged. There was freedom of religion, freedom of travel and general security throughout its dominions. Jews could settle anywhere, and in Judea their feelings were respected and they had their own priestly council to enforce the Jewish law.

Devotion to the Law was the unifying factor within Judaism, but this had come to include much more than the law given by Moses (peace be on him). There were oral traditions of Moses and other ramifications, explanations, commentaries, ritualistic details, etc., of the later Jewish prophets, rabbis and doctors of law, which had become part of the Jewish canon. At the time of Jesus (peace be on him), there were many religious factions among the Jews. While all Jews subscribed to the authority of the Torah and the sacrificial services of the Temple, beyond that sectarian differences arose as to how these tenets of faith should be interpreted in daily life. The two main groups were known as Saducees and Pharisees. Much of the preaching of Jesus was directed at them, for their emphasis on fulfilling the 'letter of the Law' without its spirit created in their religious life a blind formalism in which sincerity and humility were lacking. Jesus even pointed out that although they followed the most minute details of the Law scrupulously, many of their religious observances were acts of hypocrisy, performed so that they would be seen and praised by others rather than for the sake of God alone.

The Early Life of Jesus

Mary (Miriam), the mother of Jesus (peace be on him), was the first-born of 'Imran, a descendant of Aaron. Before Mary's birth, her mother dedicated the child whom she was carrying to the service of God. As a girl Mary was placed under the guardianship of Zachariah (peace be on him), a prophet of God, a priest and the father of John the Baptist (Yahya). The story of the annunciation to Mary of the child she would bear and of the birth of Jesus is related very movingly in the Qur'an:

"Then We sent to her our angel, and he appeared before her as a man in all respects. She said: 'I seek refuge from thee to (God) Most Gracious! (Come not near) if thou dost fear God.' He said: 'I am but a messenger from thy Sustainer (to announce) to thee the gift of a holy son.' She said: 'How shall I have a son, seeing that no man has touched me, and I am not unchaste.' He said: 'So (it will be): thy Sustainer has said: "That is easy for Me; and that We may appoint him as a sign unto men and a mercy from Us, it is a matter decreed." '
So she conceived him, and withdrew with him to a distant place. And the pains of childbirth drove her to the trunk of a palm-tree. She said: 'If only I had died before this and had become a thing forgotten!' But (a voice) cried to her from beneath the (palm-tree): 'Do not grieve! for thy Sustainer hath provided a stream near thee; and shake toward thyself the trunk of the palm-tree. It will let fall fresh ripe dates upon thee. So eat and drink and be comforted.' " (19:17-26)

Thus Jesus (peace be on him) was born from a virgin mother. This is an indication that God creates what He pleases and in whatever way He likes, and no implication of divinity is involved. One may also recall the birth of Isaac (peace be on him) when his mother Sarah was extremely old.

Later Mary married a carpenter named Joseph, who was a descendant of David, and had other children. We may suppose that Jesus (peace be on him), as the oldest son, learned the art of carpentry from Joseph and after his death may have been the chief support of the family. He shared with his mother the cares of the household as a devoted son ("He has enjoined on me . . .to cherish my mother" - Qur'an 19:32). As a carpenter, he came in direct contact with the daily labors and domestic

57

life of his neighbors, sharing their sorrows and joys, and this is reflected in his later parables.

Qur'an tells us that Jesus (peace be on him) received inspiration from God at a very early age, while he was still an infant. Later, at home and in the synagogue, he became familiar with the religious traditions of his people.

"And He will impart to him revelation, and wisdom, and the *Taurat*, and the *Injil* [revelation to Jesus] . . ." (3:48)

John the Baptist (Yahya)

In 26 or 27 A.C., John the Baptist (Yahya, peace be on him), a cousin of Jesus who is also mentioned in Qur'an as being a prophet of God, began his ministry. From the New Testament we learn that his message was a call to national repentance. He set forth a severe standard of moral conduct, of fasting and simplicity in food and dress as a condition of repentance, an inner purification rather than external rites. All who hoped to be forgiven for their sins should show the genuineness of their penitence by receiving baptism, a symbol of a complete break with the past. Yahya called for charity, honesty and sincerity of spirit as opposed to the selfishness, greed and hypocrisy of the 'religious' men of his day. He had a popular influence and people flocked to him. The New Testament reports that Jesus (peace be on him) also came to receive his baptism at his hand. Yahya's message roused the people to such an extent that the Roman governor, Herod, became alarmed at the threat to his power and imprisoned him. Eventually he was beheaded.

The Prophethood of Jesus

The New Testament tells us that after Yahya's imprisonment, Jesus (peace be on him) went into the wilderness for a period of solitude and meditation during which he received from God a clear awareness of his mission, which was an extension of Yahya's. At that time he was probably in his early thirties. He returned to begin his ministry of teaching and preaching to his people. Both Qur'an and the New Testament Gospels confirm the fact that Jesus regarded himself as a messenger sent only to the Jews rather than to all mankind, to confirm the message of earlier prophets and to call his people back to obedience to the guidance given through Moses (peace be on him) and the spirit of humility and sincerity before God. Thus Qur'an says:

> "It was We Who revealed the *Taurat* (to Moses); therein was guidance and light. By its standards the Jews were judged by the prophets, who submitted to God, by the rabbis and by the doctors of law ... And in their footsteps We sent Jesus, son of Mary, confirming the *Taurat* that had come before him. We sent him the *Injil* [revelation to Jesus]; therein was guidance and light, and a confirmation of the *Taurat* that had come before him, a guidance and an admonition to those who remain conscious of God." (5:47,49)

> "And He will impart to him revelation, and wisdom, and the *Taurat*, and the *Inji*, and will make him an apostle to the Children of Israel." (3:51)

God bestowed many miraculous gifts on Jesus (peace be on him), such as healing the sick and raising the dead (3:49, 5:113) so that people might know that he was a messenger of God. The teachings of Jesus will be discussed in one of the following sections.

Concerning the later life and the death of Jesus (peace be on him) we know nothing. The story of the crucifixion, resurrection and ascension, as described in the New Testament Gospels, has been called into question and considered unbelievable even by many modern Biblical scholars, and Qur'an tells us:

> "[God punished the followers of the Old Testament for] their boast: 'We killed Christ Jesus, son of Mary, the messenger of God!' But they did not kill him nor crucify him, but it was made to appear so to them; and those who differ in this matter are indeed confused, with no (certain) knowledge, and following mere conjecture. For, of a certainty, they did not kill him: nay, God exalted him unto Himself - and God is indeed Almighty, Wise." (4:157-158)

The Problem of the New Testament Gospels

Among the twenty-seven books of the New Testament, the first four (the Gospel According to Matthew, the Gospel

According to Mark, the Gospel According to Luke, and the Gospel According to John) are referred to, collectively, as the Four Gospels. The word 'gospel' ('*injil*' in Arabic) means 'glad tidings'. In Qur'an, the word *Injil* is used exclusively to denote the revelation of God to Jesus (see 5:47, 49 and 3:51 above). Whether this revelation was ever preserved in the form of a written book only God knows. Nothing in the New Testament suggests that Jesus (peace be on him) ever wrote anything or dictated anything to his disciples. In any case, one should not confuse the *Injil* referred to in Qur'an with the Four Gospels of the New Testament. These were written at a later date (the earliest of them, Mark, around 70 A.C.) outside Palestine, in a language different from that of Jesus, by the four chroniclers Matthew, Mark, Luke and John. It may also be mentioned that there are other gospels, such as the Gospel of Barnabas and the Gospel of Infancy, which are not included in the Christian canon. The exact words spoken by Jesus are irretrievably lost, and we are left only with some glimpses of his teachings as filtered through the minds of the New Testament writers.

How much can we depend on the Four Gospels as a biography of Jesus (peace be on him) and as a record of his teachings? The results of the researches and textual criticisms carried out over the last two centuries by Biblical scholars (see references [2] and [3] for a comprehensive treatment) is summarized as follows by H. G. Good in the opening paragraph of his article, "The Life and Teaching of Jesus" in [2]: "Today we realize that the life of Jesus can never be written. The material is wanting. Neither in quality nor in extent do the gospels satisfy the requirements of a modern biography. At best they offer us certain memorabilia of the public ministry of Jesus, hardly adequate to construct the story of the year or years during which he evangelized his people, and barely sufficing to mirror the chief features of his message."

It is clear that if the Muslim traditionists (*Muhaddithin*) had been presented with material similar to what is reported in the Gospels, they would have rejected it without a second thought because of lack of any documentation, even before trying to apply the criterion of credibility (see Unit 9: Qur'an and Hadith, p. 10, for criteria for accepting a report concerning

Prophet Muhammad).   Even the biographers of Prophet Muhammad (peace be on him), such as Ibn Ishaq, discarded all 'folklore' - type traditions, which constitute the entire content of the Four Gospels. We thus see that if one were to make a comparison between the Gospels and some counterpart from among the writings of Islam, we would place the Gospels somewhere below the books of *Sirah* (biography of the Prophet). A comparison of the Gospels with Qur'an or even with the weakest collections of *Hadith* is entirely absurd and shows utter ignorance either of the Gospels or of Qur'an and *Hadith* or of both.

The Teachings of Jesus

Keeping in mind the above limitations of the Gospels, we shall try to extract from them the basic message of Jesus (peace be on him) as contained in his parables or sayings. The parables of Jesus, although not reported in his own spoken words, have a ring of authenticity and accuracy, and all Biblical scholars agree on this point. We as Muslims also find them acceptable as his prophetic teachings, since they basically agree with what Qur'an reports concerning his message.

> "[Jesus said] : 'And (I have come) to confirm the truth of whatever there still remains of the *Taurat*, and to make lawful to you some of the things which (earlier) were forbidden to you. And I have come to you with a message from your Sustainer; remain, then, conscious of God and pay heed to me. Verily, God is my Sustainer as well as your Sustainer, so worship Him (alone): this is the straight way.' And when Jesus became aware of their refusal to acknowledge the truth, he asked: 'Who will be my helpers in God's cause?' The Disciples replied: 'We shall be (thy) helpers (in the cause) of God. We believe in God, and bear thou witness that we are Muslims [that is, those who submit to God].' "
> (3:50-52)

Turning now to the first three Gospels (the Gospel of John being considered quite remote from historical reality), we summarize the teachings of Jesus (peace be on him) as reported in them.

Like all other messengers of God, Jesus (peace be on him) taught his followers to worship One God and to remain conscious of Him. To impress upon them that God is a living reality rather than a theological concept, he drew their attention to natural phenomena, great or small: the beautiful 'clothing' of the lillies (Matt. 6:28), the feeding of the ravens (Luke 2:24), the hairs of a man's head (Matt. 10:29). God is the Lord of the Universe (Matt. 11:25). His sovereignty has no limits (Mark 10:27, 12:24). God, as Ruler, is also Judge. On the appointed Day, each shall receive from God the reward of his deeds according to the most precise reckoning (Matt. 24:45 ff, 24:14ff).

A mere belief in God is not enough; one must have a complete trust in Him. God is like a Father to mankind (Matt. 5:45, Luke 6:36) in his care and love for us (Matt. 6:11, 6:26, 10:29, Luke 12:6 ff, 12:24 ff), and all our support and help depends on Him. It is clear that Jesus' use of the word 'Father' ('*Abba*') did not involve the corresponding term 'son', as the Christian evangelists Paul and John have interpreted it. The word 'Father' as used by Jesus is synonymous with the Quranic name '*Rab*' (the Sustainer and Cherisher) for God.

Jesus (peace be on him) taught that the humble, the meek, the penitent, the pure in heart and those who are persecuted for the sake of righteousness are among the blessed of God (Matt. 5:3-11). Those people are righteous who practice the commandements of God and teach them to others. Jesus exhorted his immediate disciples to do everything in their power to avoid evil and to do good to others. It is not enough to love your neighbor; one ought to love even his enemies and pray for his persecutors, thus striving for perfection in moral conduct. One ought not to make a show of his piety and generosity, like the hypocrites, but to purify his intentions and do these acts in prirecy, for the sake of God alone (Matt. 6:2-6).

Jesus, like John the Baptist (peace be on them) before him, emphasized to his people the necessity of repentance and reformation. As God's messenger, his mission was to confirm the truth and vitality of the earlier message and to stress the necessity of bringing back the spirit of humility and inner purification to the formal observances of the laws of the Torah. He stressed the moral rather than the ritual aspects of religion, reviving its true spirit, as opposed to adhering strictly to its rites without any inner God-consciousness or sincerity. By the forcefulness of his parables, he tried to make his people realize that nothing but sincerity of heart and purity of intentions would be acceptable to God.

The influence of the teachings of Jesus (peace be on him) on history, especially that of the West, cannot be overestimated. The Roman and Greek view of the world was purely secular, based on the premise that God (or 'gods') is not concerned with the moral conduct of men. The twofold emphasis in the teachings of Jesus on the love and mercy of God and the accountability of man to Him provided the much-needed spiritual foundation of the morality of Western society.

We as Muslims believe in the truth of all the prophets of God, and feel very close to all those who truly follow the teachings of Abraham, Moses or Jesus (peace and God's blessings be on them).

References

[1] *The New Testament*: Matthew, Mark, Luke and John.
[2] A. S. Peake, *A Commentary on the Bible*, Thomas Nelson & Sons, 1952 Edition.
[3] Charles Guignebert, *Jesus*, University Books, 1966.

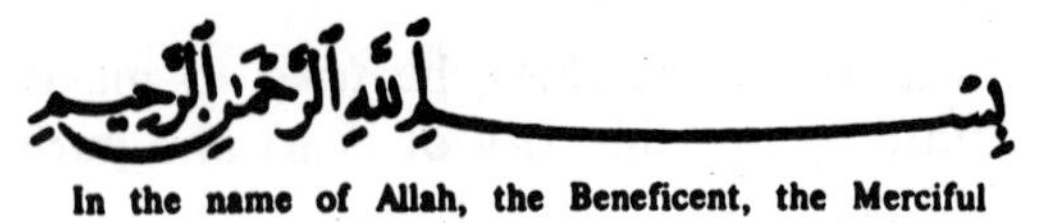

In the name of Allah, the Beneficent, the Merciful

QUR'AN

1. INTRODUCTION

Muhammad (peace be on him) was in his fortieth year, a man respected and loved by the citizens of his native city, Mecca, for his kindness, trustworthiness and uprightness of character, He was blessed with a loving wife, devoted children, and sufficient means to live comfortably. Yet he was restless. Puzzled by the mysteries of life and the universe, dissatisfied and filled with disgust at the pagan practices, the worship of idols, and the general immorality and degradation of his people, he used to retire for meditation to Hira, a cave in the hills near Mecca. One night, while he was deep in meditation, an angel appeared to him and said, "Read!" Amazed and frightened, Muhammad replied, "I do not know to read." The angel repeated his command, and again Muhammad gave the same reply. The angel came close to him and pressed him to himself, saying:

"Iqra be-isme Rabbikal ladhee khalaq,
Khalaqal insana min alaq,
Iqra wa rabbukal Akram,
al ladhi allama bil qalam —
allamal insana ma lam ya' lam."

"Read, in the name of thy Lord Who created,
created man from a clot.
Read, for thy Lord is Most Bountiful,
He Who taught (the use of) the pen —
taught man that which he knew not."   (Holy Qur'an 96:1-5)

With these words began, in the year 610 A.C. (After Christ), the revelation of the Holy Qur'an to Prophet Muhammad (peace be on him). The revelations continued during the twenty-three years of his prophethood, ending shortly before his death in 632 A.C. with the verse:

"Al yowma akmalto lakum deenakum wa

atmamto alaikum ni'mati wa radito lakum
al-Islama deena."

"This day have I perfected your religion for
you, completed my favor upon you, and have
chosen for you Islam as your religion." (5:4)

Between these first and last revealed verses unfolds a book
which, more than any single phenomenon known to us, has
fundamentally affected the religious, social and political history
of the world. Never has any other book provided to so many
people, and over so long a span of time, comprehensive answers
to the basic questions: what is the purpose of my life? how
shall I live it in order to achieve this purpose? Qur'an represents
the ultimate manifestation of God's grace to man, the ultimate
guidance, the ultimate wisdom, and the ultimate beauty of
expression — in short, the speech of God.

2.   THE COLLECTION AND PUBLICATION OF QUR'AN

There is no doubt that the Qur'an we use today is as
authentic and complete as the original Book. Serious scholars,
Muslims and non-Muslims alike, have concluded beyond question
that the present-day Qur'an is the very same Book which
Muhammad (peace be on him) received, taught, lived by and
bequeathed to humanity almost fourteen centuries ago. A few
observations may clarify this point.

(1) Prophet Muhammad (peace be on him) is reported
to have said that whenever the Angel Gabriel communicated
to him new verses of Qur'an, he would make the Prophet
repeat them as often as necessary until he knew them by
memory. The Angel Gabriel also told Muhammad the exact
position in the collection of chapters and verses of Qur'an in
which the new verses were to be placed. Thus the arrangement
of Qur'an, which is different from its order of revelation, was
prescribed by God.

(2) Since the Holy Prophet (peace be on him) himself
could neither read nor write, he dictated the revelations to one
of his Companions who could write as soon as he had received
them. Whatever his scribe recorded was read back to him for
verification. Every word was reviewed and every passage was

65

put into its proper place at the Prophet's own direction.

(3) The Arabs before and during the time of the Prophet (peace be on him) were, in general, illiterate people, but they were nevertheless great admirers of literature. The only way they were able to enjoy literary works was to memorize poems, speeches and literary passages. Thus the Companions of the Prophet hastened to memorize Qur'an, the inimitable speech of God. They recited it in resonant intonations, alone or in company, quoted its passages, and found in it the greatest satisfaction and the deepest joy. (Even today, when Qur'an is printed in millions of copies all over the world and great numbers of Muslims can read Arabic, thousands of Muslims still lovingly commit it to memory.)

There are five men among the Companions who had memorized the whole of Qur'an in the lifetime of the Prophet (peace be on him). These were: Mu'adh ibn Jabal, 'Ibada ibn al-Samat, Ubay ibn K'ab, Abu Ayub, and Abu Darda. There were others who had memorized large portions of Qur'an.

(4) Immediately after the death of the Prophet (peace be on him) in 632 A.C., Umar impressed upon Abu Bakr, the first Caliph, the urgency of compiling the entire Qur'an in one volume. Abu Bakr instructed Zaid ibn Thabit, Muhammad's chief scribe of revelation, to collect the entire Qur'an. When all the chapters were collected by Zaid, a committee was appointed to have the whole of Qur'an copied in one volume under their supervision. The committee was directed to follow the pronunciation of the Mudar tribe (one branch of which was the Qur'aish family, to which the Prophet belonged), as the Qur'an had been revealed in the language of Mudar. This standard text was reviewed by many Companions, including the five who had memorized it all, and approved by them as being complete and accurate. It was then placed in the custody of the Prophet's widow, Umar's daughter Hafsa.

(5) The second Caliph, Umar, opened many schools for the teaching of Qur'an throughout the Muslim territories. It is reported that Abu Darda, who taught in the Assembly Mosque of Damascus, alone had sixteen hundred pupils. Once the Caliph wrote to his commanders to send to Medina men who had memorized the entire Qur'an so that they could be appointed as teachers. Sa'd ibn Waqqas, his commander in

Iraq, replied that there were three hundred such persons in his army alone.

(6) It was reported to the third Caliph, Uthman, that in far-off places, some words of Qur'an were being pronounced with variants, especially by non-Arab converts to Islam. Uthman acted swiftly. He consulted the prominent Companions and appointed a committee of four members, including Zaid ibn Thabit, to meet the situation. All copies of Qur'an which were in use were recalled and replaced by copies of the standard versions (which was with Hafsa), to be recited according to the dialect of Qur'aish, the very same dialect in which Prophet Muhammad (peace be on him) himself had recited it. Apart from the orthographical marks inserted in later times to make reading and recitation easy, the Qur'an as printed today is indentical with the version authorized by Uthman and the Companions of the Prophet in 651 A.C.

From these facts, scholars have concluded that the Qur'an stands as it was dictated, recited and arranged by the Prophet (peace be on him). It is a matter of historic record that there has never been any addition to it, no omission from it, and no distortion has occurred in it, and indeed, the purity of Qur'an is pledged by God Himself:

"Certainly We have sent down the Message and assuredly We will be its guardian." (15:9)

3. THE NUMBER OF CHAPTERS AND VERSES OF QUR'AN

The Holy Qur'an is divided into 114 chapters (*surahs*), 86 of which were revealed to the Holy Prophet (peace be on him) in Mecca and 28 in Medina. The number of verses (*ayahs*) varies from chapter to chapter. The shortest chapters (103, 108 and 110) have three verses each, while the longest, *Surah* 2, contains 286 verses. The total number of verses in Qur'an is 6,239.

4. QUR'AN'S TESTIMONY ABOUT ITSELF

We find many passages in Qur'an which describe its origin, its purpose and its style. Here we summarize and reproduce a few of these verses.

(1)   Qur'an – also referred to as the Book of God (*Kitab ul-Allah*), Speech of God (*Kalam ul-Allah*), the Message (*al-Zikr*), and the Criterion (*al-Furqan*) –is the speech of God in the Arabic language, communicated to the Prophet Muhammad (peace be on him) by the Holy and Trustworthy Spirit (*Rooh al-Quds, Rooh al-Ameen*), the Angel Gabriel.

"Truly it is the revelation from the Sustainer of the worlds brought down by the Trustworthy Spirit to thy heart, that thou mayest admonish, in a clear Arabic tongue."   (26:192-195)

"Say: The Holy Spirit has brought it from thy Sustainer in truth, in order to strengthen those who believe, and as a guide and glad tidings to Muslims."   (16:102)

"We have sent it down as an Arabic Qur'an in order that you may learn wisdom."   (12:2)

(2)   Its message is conveyed in easy language.
"And indeed We have made the Qur'an easy to understand and remember.   Then, is there any who will receive admonition?"   (54:17; also 54:22, 32 and 40)

"Verily We have made it easy in thy tongue, so that they may give heed."   (44:58)

(3)   As it is the Speech of God, no part of it can be imitated by men.
"And if you are in doubt as to what We have revealed to Our servant, then produces a chapter like thereunto; and call your witnesses and helpers besides God, if your (doubts) are true.   But if you cannot –and certainly you cannot – then fear the Fire..."   (2:23-24)

It may be mentioned that some of the chapters of Qur'an consist of only three verses.   Among the contemporaries of the Holy Prophet (peace be on him) were men known to be great masters of the Arabic language and literature, and they had the most compelling motives for taking up this challenge.   But in spite of all their efforts, they were unable to produce even a few sentences like the Qur'an in content or expression.

(4)   Qur'an as we read it today is exactly the same as it was received by Prophet Muhammad (peace be on him).   God has taken it upon Himself to guard its purity.

"Certainly We have sent down the Message, and assuredly We will be its guardian."   (15:9)

"No falsehood can approach it from before it or behind it. It is
sent down by the All-Wise, the All-Praiseworthy." (41:42)

(5) Qur'an is consistent with itself, no part of it contradict-
ing another, and it explains matters clearly.

"God has revealed the most beautiful discourse in the form of a
Book, consistent with itself." (39:23)

"It is an Arabic Qur'an without any crookedness, (revealed) in
order that they may guard against evil." (39:27)

"And no question do they bring to thee [the Prophet] but We
reveal to thee the truth and the best explanation." (35:33)

(6) Qur'an is addressed to all mankind. It enlightens
people concerning God and His purposes with man. It is meant
to be a guide in this world and to give glad tidings of the Next
World to those who seek a righteous way of life.

"This is naught but a Message to all worlds, for whosoever of you
would go straight." (81:27-28)

"This is the Book, wherein is no doubt, a guidance for all the God-
conscious." (2:22)

"And We revealed the Book to thee so that thou shouldst make
clear to them the matters in which they differ, and that it should
be a guide and a mercy to the believing people." (16:64)

"A Book which We have revealed to thee, in order that thou
mightest lead mankind out of the depths of darkness into light..."
(14:1)

5. HOW TO READ QUR'AN

God says:

"Those to whom We have sent the Book study it as it should be
studied; they are the ones who believe in it; and those who reject
it, they are the losers." (2:121)

If one remembers that the Qur'an was communicated to
the Prophet (peace be on him) over a period of twenty-three
years, a little at a time, it becomes plain that it should be read
a little at a time, and that this little demands meditation
assimilation and action (if it requires action). The Prophet
instructed his Companions in this manner also.

This manner of studying Qur'an is especially recommended

to a Western reader, who is likely to approach Qur'an with the misconception that it is more or less like the Bible. This is far from being the case. Qur'an is not a history book, nor a biography, nor a collection of sayings: in fact, it does not resemble any book authored by men, including the Old and New Testaments or the books of any other religions. Qur'an is the speech of God addressed to man to be a guide for his conduct for all time to come. Its basic purpose is to instruct and to teach concerning God and His purposes with man. To teach is to explain and to repeat and to illustrate the basic principles in various ways. Qur'an's style can be compared to the work of God, i.e., nature. Nature is repetitive, yet has infinite variety; so has Qur'an. Nature is God's creation; Qur'an is God's speech — and both are limitless. As God says:

> "Though all the trees on earth were pens and the ocean (made into ink) and seven oceans behind it to replenish it, yet would not the words of God be exhausted (in the writing), for God is All-Powerful and All-Wise." (31:27)

The more we investigate natural phenomena, the more surprises there are in store for us. Similarly, the more we study Qur'an, in the light of our growing knowledge of the world and of man, the more surprises await us in the unfolding of its meaning.

6.   THE TEACHINGS OF QUR'AN

The basic objective of Qur'an is to awaken the soul of man to the awareness of the sovereignty of God in the universe and in human affairs. Everything that was or that is or that will be comes from God; there is none to share His dominion. Man is merely a trustee in the vast universe of God, and the purpose of his creation is to worship God.

To worship God does not mean to remove oneself from the activities of life in order to perform devotional acts. On the contrary, every act we perform is worship if it is done with good intentions in accordance with the laws given by God. The ultimate responsibility of each man is to God alone, and every human being will be questioned concerning what he did with God's gifts: life itself, faculties, talents, intellect, time, possessions and all that one has been given. The life of this world is of limited span, but it is the foundation on which the future Life of unlimited duration is to be built. Thus the present life is of great import and is not to be wasted.

Qur'an, then, outlines the basic principles covering the entire field of human affairs so that man may know what is expected of him. These principles cover not only personal matters, but also the relations between man and man and between one group of people and another. Excellence in this life is a pre-requisite for excellence in the future Life. Thus Qur'an exhorts people to observe, to think, to investigate, to search earnestly for truth, to strive for excellence in conduct and manners, in service to others, in seeking for justice for all and in striving for peace among the peoples of the earth. Qur'an tells man that he is the vice-gerent (deputy) of God on earth and that he should act accordingly. It asks every man to free himself from servitude to other men, from bondage to his own desires, from the shackles of false gods such as pride in birth, wealth, social status or national origin, and to attain the true dignity and wisdom which befits God's *Khalifa* (vice-gerent) on earth. To achieve these goals, it is necessary that the consciousness of the reality of God reach the innermost recesses of the mind. Qur'an speaks of God-consciousness (*taqwa*) as the basis of all good actions. To help man achieve God-consciousness, God has ordained specific acts of worship for Muslims — prayer (*salat*), fasting (*siyam*), pilgrimage (*hajj*) and poor-due (*zakat*) — as a reminder that everything we have is for God and that We shall return to Him.

7.   SELECTIONS FROM QUR'AN

(1) God

Say: He is God, One. God is the Self-Sufficient. He begets not nor is He begotten, and there is nothing comparable to Him. (112:1-4)

God! There is no god but He, the Living, the Eternal. Slumber does not overpower Him, nor sleep. To Him belongs all that is in the heavens and earth. Who is there that shall intercede with Him, except by His leave? He knows what lies before them [mankind] and what is behind them; and they do not comprehend anything

71

of His knowledge, except so much as He wills. His throne (of sovereignty) comprises the heavens and the earth; the preserving of them does not oppress Him. He is the Most High, the Almighty. (2: 255)

Among His signs is this, that He created you from dust, then behold! you are men scattered (through the earth). And among His signs is this, that He created for you spouses from among yourselves, that you may find repose in them, and He has put love and compassion between your (hearts). Surely in that are signs for those who reflect. And among His signs is the creation of the heavens and earth, and the variations in your languages and colors. Surely in that are signs for those who know. (30:20-22)

Whatever is in the heavens and on earth declares the praises and glory of God — the Sovereign, the Holy One, the Exalted in Might, the Wise. It is He Who has sent amongst the unlettered an apostle from among themselves, to rehearse to them His signs, to sanctify them, and to instruct them in scripture and wisdom, — although they had been, before, in manifest error — as well as (to confer all these benefits upon) others of them, who have not already joined them, and He is Exalted in Might, Wise. Such is the bounty of God, which He bestows on whom He will: and God is the Lord of the highest bounty. (62:2-4)

(2) Man

Has there not been a period of time when man was nothing — (not even) mentioned? Verily We created man from a drop of sperm, mingled, in order to try him; so We gave him (the gifts of) hearing and sight. We showed him the way; whether he be grateful or ungrateful (rests with him). (76:1-3)

Fair in the eyes of men is the love of things they covet: women and sons, heaped-up hoards of gold and silver, horses branded, and cattle, and well-tilled land. Such are the possessions of this world's life; but in nearness to God is the best of goals. (3:14)

Man can have nothing except what he strives for. (53:39)

And He made you vice-gerents on earth, and He raised some of you, in ranks, above others, so that He may try you in the gifts He has given you. Verily thy Sustainer is quick in punishment, yet He is indeed Oft-Forgiving, and Most Merciful. (6:165)

(3) Righteousness

Those who spend freely [for charity] whether in prosperity or in adversity; who control anger, and pardon people; and God loves those who do good to others. (3:134)

O you who believe! Stand out firmly for justice, as witnesses to God, even as against yourselves, or your parents, or your kin, and whether it concerns rich or poor, for God can best protect both. (4:135)

It is not righteousness that you turn your faces to the east and the west [when you pray]. True righteousness is this: to believe in God, and the Last Day, the angels, the Book and the prophets; to spend of one's substance, out of love for Him, for kinsmen, orphans, the needy and the traveller, and for the ransom of captives; to be regular in prayers [*salat*] and to pay the poor-due [*zakat*]; to fulfill the contracts which you have made, and endure with fortitude pain, hardship and peril. These are they who are true in their faith, these are the truly God-fearing. (2:177)

(4) Supplications

All praise is due to God, the Sustainer of the Worlds, the Merciful, the Mercy-giving, Master of the Day of Judgment. Thee alone do we worship and from Thee alone do we ask help. Show us the straight path, the path of those upon whom is Thy favor, who have not deserved Thy anger, and who have not gone astray. (1:1-7)

Our Sustainer! Do not take us to task if we forget or make a mistake. Our Sustainer! Do not charge us with a burden like that which Thou didst lay upon those before us. Our Sustainer! Do not lay on us a burden greater than we have strength to bear. Blot out our sins, forgive us, and have mercy on us. Thou art our Protector; help us against the people who reject faith. (2:286)

HADITH

1. THE MEANING OF 'SUNNAH' AND 'HADITH'

The Arabic word *'sunnah'* means 'the practice.' Accordingly, we find that in Qur'an God says: "You will find no change in the practice of God (*sunnat Allah*)" (33:62). The word *'hadith'* means 'a saying' or 'a report,' and thus refers to a quotation or to an account of what happened. In common usage, these words are applied particularly to Prophet Muhammad's practices and way of life *(sunnah)* and to the reports of what he did or said (*hadith*).

Sunnah refers actually to *those practices of the Prophet (peace be on him) which are a part of his prophetic mission, not mere incidentals, and which were followed by his Companions.* Thus, the order in which *wudu* (ablution) is performed and the way in which we pray (*salat*) are examples of *sunnah*, while to live in Medina or to ride a camel are not. Prophet Muhammad used to make a clear distinction between those of his actions which were to be followed by Muslims (i.e., *sunnah*) and those which were not. A *sunnah* is transmitted from one person to another through observation and imitation or through instruction.

A *hadith* is a report or a verbal tradition, transmitted by word of mouth, of what the Prophet (peace be on him) said or did, or his reaction to something said or done by others. There could be examples of *sunnah* (the Prophet's practice) for which there is no *hadith* (verbal expression of the Prophet), and, of course, there are hundreds of *hadiths* (for example, concerning the good qualities of the Prophet's Companions or the attributes of God) which contain no report about *sunnah*. A Companion of the Prophet who had heard him say something or seen him do something reported it to others, who in turn reported it to others, and so on. When, at a later date, collections of *hadiths* (or *ahadith*, the Arabic plural) were compiled, each report was prefaced by a chain of transmitters (*isnad*), for example: "A reported that B reported that C reported that Umar bin al-Khattab reported God's Messenger as saying...," as well as the text (*matn*). In this way the compilers of these books provided not only the information which was reported about the Prophet but also its documentation. Every *hadith* must have an *isnad* as well as a *matn*. Since now the canonical books of *hadith* are widely available in print, we can freely quote the text of a *hadith* without mentioning the *isnad*.

2. THE IMPORTANCE OF SUNNAH AND HADITH

When a great man dies, people want to know as much as possible about his life and works. To satisfy this need, many people who have had the privilege of associating with him, such as his family, relatives, friends, co-workers, acquaintances, and even those who saw him only from a distance, report what they saw him do or heard him say. In the case of Prophet Muhammad (peace be on him), the reporting of his deeds and words was not merely for the sake of curiosity or for historical record but, much more significantly, also as a legal basis for the Islamic practice of Muslims for all time to come. The Prophet's status for Muslims as an example to be followed, as a judge and as an exponent of God's injunctions, is clearly expressed in the following verses of Qur'an:

"You have indeed in the Messenger of God an excellent example (of conduct)." (33:21)

"He who obeys the Prophet obeys God." (4:80)

"For (the Prophet) commands them what is just and forbids them what is evil. He allows them as lawful what is good and prohibits them from what is bad." (7:157)

"And We have sent down unto thee [the Prophet] the message, that thou mayest explain clearly to men what is sent for them and that they may give thought." (14:44)

It is thus clear that first Qur'an and then *Sunnah* are the basis of Islamic law (*Shari'ah*). This was recognized by all the Companions of the Prophet (peace be on him), all the Muslim jurists, and by all the generations of Muslims who followed them.

3.   CANONICAL BOOKS OF HADITH

From the very beginning, the Companions of the Prophet (peace be on him) were extremely eager to know what the Prophet did and said so that they might follow his example and injunctions. After his death, when Islam spread far and wide, new Muslims were also eager to hear all about him and to follow his example. His Companions were listened to eagerly and, in the course of time, a great amount of material concerning the Prophet became current. While this was conveyed largely by word of mouth, some persons made small collections of these traditions for their own use. These could hardly be called books, but the material they contained was included in later works. A few books were written on the life of the Prophet (*sirah*), but the authors of these works did not use the strict principles of research and documentation which characterize the books of *hadith*. The purpose of these biographical works was to tell the story of the Prophet's life, while the main purpose of a book of *hadith* was to provide reference material for judges, jurists, doctors of law and, in general, for all Muslims. Obviously a reference book is different from a biography not only in its organization but also in that it requires far more stringent criteria for accepting a tradition. These criteria will be described in Section 4. The most authoriative books of *hadith* are the following two:

(1)   the *Sahih* of Bukhari (194-256 A.H.) and

(2)   the *Sahih* of Muslim (202-261 A.H.),

the work of Bukhari being the superior of the two in its method of classification. In addition, four other books are also recognized as authoriative (completing "The Accurate Six" books of *hadith*). These are known as the *Sunan* of

(3)   Abu Daud (202-275 A.H.),

(4)   Tirmidhi (died 279 A.H.),

(5)   Nisai (215-303 A.H.), and

(6)   Ibn Majah (209-273 A.H.).

It is important to note that none of the books of *hadith*, including "The Accurate Six," were commissioned by any authoritative body, as no such body exists in Islam. They were collected on the initiative of the Compilers. Each one of them had to be critically examined and accepted by the community before being recognized as an authoritative work. This applied to the works of Bukhari and Muslim, just as it did to the others.

4. THE CRITERIA FOR ACCEPTING THE VERACITY OF A HADITH

The vast number of traditions reported to come from the Prophet (peace be on him) made it necessary to adopt certain criteria regarding their authenticity. For example, Bukhari, in compiling his work, said he had collected 600,000 traditions, and yet he included only 7,275 altogether in his *Sahih*, a total which is said to be reduced only 4,800 out of 500,000 traditions in his *Sunan*. It should be understood, however, that when one speaks of 600,000 traditions, this does not mean that number of separate items of information. As mentioned previously, each *hadith* has two parts: (1) chain of transmission (*isnad*) and (2) text (*matn*). If, therefore, the same text was found with, say, three different *isnads,* it would be counted as three *hadiths.* Even making allowances for repetitions, it is still obvious that a vast number of traditions were discarded by reputable traditionists (*muhaddithin*). What was known as *ilm-al-hadith* (the Science of Hadith) gradually developed. The following criteria were laid down to establish the the authenticity of each tradition:

The first principle of the traditionists was to verify that the chain of transmitters (*isnad*) reached back to a person who himself was present at the event being described. Secondly, he examined the life and character of each person in this chain to establish how truthful he was, what his activities and interests were, how he conducted himself, how good his memory was, how well he understood what he observed or heard, whether he was reliable or unreliable, learned or illiterate, and so on. Thousands of traditionists (*muhaddithin*) spent their lives to gather every detail of the lives of the transmitters of traditions about the Holy Prophet (peace be on him). Due to their painstaking researches, the science of *isma-ar-rijal* (Critical Biography) developed to such an extent that through them one can learn about the lives of at least 100,000 persons involved in reporting *hadiths.* The reasons for this very strict screening of reports (and the reporters) about the Prophet are quite obvious, and also have their basis in the verse.

"O you who believe! If some immoral person brings a piece of news, investigate it thoroughly. . ." (49:6)

After the reliability and truthfulness of the transmitters had been established, the next principle was to apply the the criterion of credibility or believability. The criteria for rejecting a tradition as not being credible include the following:

(1) It is against Qur'an or *Sunnah* or sound *hadiths;*
(2) It ascribes nonsense to the Prophet (peace be on him);
(3) It is against well-known evidence;
(4) It contradicts observational facts;
(5) It reports an event such that if it had occurred, hundreds of people would have observed it, while there is only one person who actually reported it;
(6) It contains vulgar words;
(7) It contains prophecies of future events with specific dates;
(8) It threatens great punishment for small errors;
(9) It promises great rewards for minor deeds.

It should be mentioned that all these criteria were derived from the examples set by the Companions of the Prophet (peace be on him). For example, during the Caliphate of Umar, a woman named Fatima bint Qais told Umar that when her husband divorced her, the Prophet did not tell him to provide her alimony. Umar said, "We cannot leave the Book of God and the *Sunnah* of the Prophet on the report of a woman, about whom we do not know whether she remembered or forgot." Again, on hearing a tradition reported on the authority of Ibn-Umar, Aisha did not accept it and remarked, "You or your transmitters do not tell lies, but sometimes one misunderstands."

5. CLASSIFICATION OF HADITHS

Hadiths have commonly been divided into three main groups:

(1) *Sahih* (sound),

(2) *Hasan* (good),

(3) *Da'if* (weak) or *Saqim* (infirm).

All the *hadiths* given by Bukhari and Muslim are considered *sahih* (sound), as are those which are not given by Bukhari and Muslim but which nevertheless fulfill the conditions laid down by either or both of these two *muhaddithin.* *Hasan* (good) traditions are those whose source is known and whose transmitters (*isnad*) are well-known for their reliability and accuracy, and these traditions are accepted by most of the learned and made use of by the doctors of law, judges and jurists.

While *hasan* (good) traditions have been recognized as a valid basis for legal decisions in Muslim systems of jurisprudence, this cannot apply to *da'if* (weak) traditions; but all traditions called *da'if* are not rejected. Those which exhort people to do good or which narrate incidents may be quoted. Abu Daud quite often used *da'if* traditions when he could find nothing better to illustrate the point with which he was dealing.

There are various grades of *da'if* traditions, which include those which may on occasion be quoted, those with links in the transmission (*isnad*) missing, and the extreme situation of improperly reported or entirely fabricated traditions.

There are other technical terms which are also used in describing various kinds of traditions, such as *gharib* (referring to the use of rare words in traditions), *mauquf* (when the *isnad* stops at one of the Companions and does not trace the tradition back to the Prophet), and so on.

6. THE CONTENTS OF HADITH

The subject matter of *hadith* is very comprehensive, dealing with almost every topic on which guidance might be sought. Bukhari divided his *Sahih* into 97 books:

3 on the beginning of revelation, faith and knowledge;

30 concerned with ablutions, prayer, poor-due, pilgrimage and fasting;

22 concerned business, trusteeship, employment and legal matters;

3 on *jihad* (striving and fighting in the path of God) and
and *dhimmies* (non-Muslim subjects);
1 on creation;
4 on the prophets and the good qualities of the Companions;
1 on the Prophet's career in Medina;
2 concerning commentaries on Qur'anic passages;
3 on marriage, divorce and maintenance of the family;
26 dealing with various matters, such as food, drink, clothing, manners, vows, etc.

Book 96 in Bukhari's *Sahih* stresses the importance of adhering to Qur'an and *Sunnah*, and the last book, which is fairly
lengthy, deals with the Oneness of God.

7. SOME SOUND HADITHS

(1) Faith

Faith has over seventy branches, the most excellent of which
is the declaration that "there is no deity but God," and the
humblest of which is the removal of what is injurious from
the road. And modesty is a branch of faith.

The Muslim is he from whose tongue and hand the Muslims
are safe.

If anyone observes our form of prayer, faces in the direction
of Ka'aba [while praying] and eats what we kill, that one is
a Muslim who has protection from God and His messenger;
so do not betray God's protection.

Abu Huraira reported that an Arab came to the Prophet and
said, "Guide me to a deed by doing which I shall enter
Paradise." The Prophet said, "Worship God and do not
associate anything with Him, observe the prescribed prayer,
pay the obligatory *zakat*, and fast during Ramadan." The
Arab replied, "By Him in Whose hand is my soul, I shall not
add anything to it nor fall short of it." Then when he turned
away, the Prophet said, "If anyone wishes to look at a man
who will be among the people of Paradise, let him look at this
man" [i.e., if anyone fulfills his essential obligations completely,
without falling short of them in any way, he will enter

Paradise even if he does nothing none].

When I issue any command to you regarding your religion, accept it; but when I say something to you based on my opinion, I am merely a human being.

I am leaving two things among you after my death. If you stick to them firmly, you will never go astray from the right path. One is the Holy Qur'an and the other is my *Sunnah* [conduct and way of living].

(2) Knowledge

Two people only may be envied: a man to whom God has given property, and he disposes of it on what is right; and a man to whom God has given wisdom, who acts according to it and teaches it.

He who goes out in search of knowledge is in the path of God until he returns.

Be on your guard about tradition from me, except what you know; for he who lies about me deliberately will certainly come to his abode in Hell.

The best and greatest among you is he who learns the Holy Qur'an and teaches it to others.

(3) Prayer

Ibn Mas'ud said: "I asked the Prophet which action is dearest to God, and he replied, 'Prayer at its proper time.' I asked what came next, and he replied that it was kindness to parents. I asked what came next, and he replied that it was *jihad* [striving] in God's path.

What lies between a man and disbelief is the abandoment of prayer.

(4) Moderation

The acts most pleasing to God are those which are done most regularly, even if they amount to little.

Choose such actions as you are capable of performing, for God does not grow weary, but you do.

(5) Work

After observing everything enjoined by God, it is one's first and foremost duty to provide a legal and honest living.

إِنَّ الصَّلٰوةَ
كَانَتْ عَلَى الْمُؤْمِنِينَ كِتَابًا مَوْقُوتًا

For such prayers are enjoined on Believers at stated times. (Qur'an 4:103)

To God belong the East and the West.

(Qur'an 2:115

وَاَنْ لَّيْسَ لِلْاِنْسَانِ اِلَّا مَا سَعَى

And that man can have nothing but what he strives for.
(Qur'an 53:39)

DEFINITIONS AND KEY WORDS

1. *Salat* = formal prayers of Muslims, observed at fixed times and occasions.
2. *Du'a* = informal, personal prayer (Supplication).
3. *Wudu* = ablution performed by washing exposed parts of the body, a necessary preparation for prayers (*salat*).
4. *Tayammum* = dry cleansing, with clean earth, sand or on a clean surface instead of ablution (*wudu*) when circumstances make it necessary.
5. *Ghusl* = complete bathing from head to foot.
6. *Fajr* = the dawn prayer
7. *Dhur* = the early afternoon prayer
8. *'Asr* = the late afternoon prayer ⎱ the five daily
9. *Maghrib* = the evening prayer ⎰ prayers
10. *'Isha* = the night prayer
11. *Qibla* = the direction of Ka'aba in Mecca.
12. *Rakat* = unit of which each prayer (*salat*) consists.
13. *Surah* = chapter of Qur'an.
14. *Al Fateha* = the opening *surah* of Qur'an.
15. *Fard* (prayers) = the required (prayers), prescribed in Qur'an.
16. *Sunnah* (prayers)= additional, supererogatory (prayers) according to the practice of Prophet Muhammad (peace be on him).
17. *Imam* = the person who leads a congregational prayer.
18. *Adhan* = the call to prayers (*salat*).
19. *Jum'a* (prayer) = Friday (prayer).
20. *Eid* = festival.
21. *Takbir* = recitation of the words *"Allahu Akbar"* (God is Most Great).
22. *Khutba* = sermon

God is the Greatest

الله اكبر

God is the Greatest

الله اكبر

1. INTRODUCTION

Among the Five Pillars of Islam, Prayer (*Salat*) is the second, the first being Faith *(Iman)*. Fasting (*Sawm*) is observed for one month each year, the Poor-due (*Zakat*) is given once a year, and the Pilgrimage (*Hajj*) is performed once in a lifetime, but prayers (*salat*) are five times a day — at dawn, in the early after-noon, in the late afternoon, just after sunset, and at night. The essence of Islam is consciousness of and submission to God, and the most direct means of developing these qualities is through prayer. It is clear that prayer once a week or even once a day is not enough, as we become so absorbed in our activities that we tend to forget our Creator. That is why prayers (*salat*) are prescribed five times each day.

It may seem difficult at times to observe all the prayers regularly, but to those who are humble before their Creator and who believe that they shall meet Him after death, it is a joy and a pleasure. This is expressed in the Qur'an thus:

"Seek help in patience and prayer. This is indeed hard except to those who are humble, who bear in mind that they shall meet their Lord and that they are to return to Him." (2:45-46)

The Islamic prayers (*salat*), like any prayers, have a certain form, a series of actions and recitations, and this has a signifi-cance which will be discussed later; but the motions and the words are not the essence of the prayers. The essence of the prayers, indeed of all forms of Islamic worship (Poor-due, Fasting, Pilgrimage), is the spirit of humility and submission to God. This spirit may not be present every time we pray, but with or without it, we should observe all the prayers. It is obvious that if one never prays or prays only seldom, he is not likely to attain the spirit of submission. In fact, the neglect of prayer (*salat*) gradually leads one to feel and to act as if he does not believe in God or in the life hereafter, although he may profess otherwise. On the other hand, one who starts observing prayers regularly may attain, by degrees and stages, a feeling of being present before his Lord, a sense of peace in his heart, a firm criterion of right and wrong in his attitudes and actions, and the spirit of true submission. He will never lose sight of the fact that he is only a human being of limited capacities, living on this earth for a short while, and that his Lord is the Almighty Creator and Sustainer of the universe, Who gave him his life and to Whom he will return. He will become watchful not to go beyond the limits set by God, and he will develop whatever is good in himself and suppress his wrong inclinations and wishes. In time, he should attain such a sharp criterion of good and evil that all his actions follow, in an easy and natural way, whatever is good, noble and worth striving for.

These statements are only an elaboration of what is said to us in Qur'an about prayers (*salat*):

"O you who believe! seek help with patient perseverance and prayer; for God is with those who patiently persevere." (2:153)

"Those who believe, and whose hearts find satisfaction in the remembrance of God: for without doubt by the remembrance of God hearts are refreshed." (13:28)

"Establish regular prayers — at the sun's decline till the darkness of the night, and the recitation of the dawn prayer: surely the recitation of the dawn prayer is witnessed. And as for the night, keep vigil a part of it, as a work of superrogation [doing more than duty requires] for thee: It may be that thy Lord will raise thee up to a praiseworthy station." (17:78-79)

"...and proclaim the praises of thy Lord before the rising of the sun, and before its setting; and proclaim thy Lord's praises in the watches of the night, and at the ends of the day: that thou mayest have (spiritual) joy." (20:130)

"So glory be to God, when you reach eventide and when you rise at dawn — His is the praise in the heavens and on earth — and in the late afternoon when the day begins to decline." (30:17-18)

"And be steadfast in prayer and regular in charity: and whatever good you send forth for your souls before you,

89

you shall find it with God: for God sees well all that you do." (2:110)

It should be borne in mind that God does not need our prayers, for He is above all needs. God's authority over the universe, including all human affairs, is not decreased in the least even if no man acknowledges Him or prays to Him. He does not require our prostrations or our words of praise to add to His majesty and glory. The prayers are for ourselves, for our own spiritual good, in harmony with our own natural instinct to proclaim God's glory and to bow down before Him in thankfulness and praise.

The Islamic form of prayer (*salat*) achieves these instinctive aspirations to the utmost extent. We wash ourselves (*wudu*), which not only cleans and refreshes us but also prepares us mentally for the act of prayer. We stand before God, seeking His guidance and help, and ask Him again and again to show us the straight path. We recite from His Book and refresh our belief in His mercy and goodness, in the fact that we will one day return to Him to give an accounting of ourselves, in the moral teachings of Qur'an and in the truth of His messenger Muhammad (peace be on him). The bowing and prostration are the very embodiment of the spirit of humility and submission to God.

Prayers (*salat*) are also an expression of brotherhood and equality among men. In a congregational prayer, we stand shoulder to shoulder with our fellow-worshippers, without distinction of social or economic status, race or color, and perform with the leader the various movements, prostrating ourselves together as one body before God. This creates among Muslims a bond of love and mutual respect which transcends all worldly considerations.

We perform the sequence of actions and recitations, both in our ablutions and in our prayers, in the way in which our Prophet (peace be on him) performed them. All Muslims throughout the world pray in the same manner in which the Prophet prayed, thus witnessing to the fact that all Muslims are one community, the community of God and His messenger.

We will now describe the actual from in which prayers (*salat*) are performed.

2. ABLUTION (WUDU), DRY CLEANSING (TAYAMMUM) AND COMPLETE BATHING (GHUSL)

Before our prayers (*salat*), we wash the exposed parts of our bodies *(wudu)*. First we silently say that our intention *(niyat)* in washing is to make *wudu*. Then we make our *wudu* in the following sequence: (1) Wash hands three times; (2) rinse mouth three times; (3) clean nostrils three times by sniffing in and blowing out water from one cupped hand; (4) wash face with both hands three times; (5) wash arms up to the elbow three times, the right arm before the left; (6) wipe top of head with wet hands, ears with thumb and forefinger, and neck with backs of wet hands once; (7) wash feet up to the ankles three times, right foot first. When the *wudu* is completed, we are ready for prayers.

It is not necessary to make ablution *(wudu)* for every prayer unless during the interval between two prayers you have performed any toilet function, passed gas, vomited or slept. In these cases a repetition of *wudu* is required before your next prayer. It is also not necessary to wash your feet again if you had on thick socks after the first *wudu* of the day, but the feet are to be washed once a day for prayers.

In case of sickness in which it would be harmful to use water or when water is scarce or not available, you can substitute a dry cleansing (*tayammum*) for ablution (*wudu*). For *tayammum*, you strike your hands lightly on a clean wall or on clean earth or sand, and wipe your face with them once. Then you again strike your hands on the clean surface and wipe each arm up to the elbow once, right arm first. This is a symbolic act of conforming to God's ordinance of cleanliness as a condition for prayers and again has the effect of preparing ourselves mentally for prayers (*salat*).

In the practice of the Prophet *(Sunnah)* we find great emphasis on cleanliness. Therefore to bathe quite frequently is obviously desirable from every standpoint. Besides our ordinary bathing or showering, there are a few specific occasions when a full bath (*ghusl*) from head to foot is prescribed before one comes to prayers (*salat*). These are following marital intercourse, following an emission of semen during sleep, after the menstrual period is complete, and at the end of the discharge following childbirth. It is also recommended in the *Sunnah* to have a bath before Friday (*Jum'a*) prayer and on the two *Eids*.

It may be noted here that women are excused from prayers (*salat*) during menstruation and for forty days after childbirth.

. All these practices are performed in keeping with the the *Sunnah* (practice) of the Prophet (peace be on him) or, in the case of women, according to the Prophet's instructions.

3. DRESS

For prayers (*salat*) the Prophet (peace be on him) enjoined that men and boys should be covered at least from the navel to the knee. The head may be covered or uncovered, and the shoes are always removed. For women, the Prophet recommended that they should be covered from head to foot, leaving only the face and hands uncovered.

4. A CLEAN PLACE

We want to ensure that the place where we will pray will be reasonably clean, and it is desirable (but not essential) to provide some sort of covering, at least for the spot where our foreheads will touch the floor or ground during prostration. A napkin, handkerchief, towel, sheet or small rug will suffice for for this purpose. In Muslim countries rugs are available for prayers, but this is only a matter of convenience, not of necessity.

5. THE PRAYERS (SALAT)

Before going through the complete sequence of the prayers, there are three things to bear in mind:

A. Each of the five daily prayers consists of either two, three or four units (*rakats*), which will be described later.

B. The names of the five daily prayers, their times and the number of units (*rakats*) in each are as follows:

(1) *Fajr* (the dawn prayer), to be observed some time between dawn and sunrise, consists of two units (*rakats*), both of which are said aloud.

(2) *Dhur* (the early afternoon prayer), to be observed some time just after noon until mid-afternoon, consists of four *rakats*, all of which are said silently.

(3) *'Asr* (the late afternoon prayer), to be observed some time between mid-afternoon and sunset, consists of four *rakats*, all of which are said silently.

(4) *Maghrib* (the evening prayer), to be observed some time just after sunset until the last light fades, consists of three *rakats*, of which the first two are said aloud and the third is said silently.

(5) *'Isha* (the night prayer), to be observed at some time during the night, consists of four *rakats*, of which the first two are said aloud and the last two silently.

C. There are four basic positions which we assume during our prayers, which are illustrated by the photos on this and the following pages. These positions are:

(1) Standing (*iqamah*), with the right hand clasped lightly above the left, wrist over wrist, and held a little above the waist (Photo 3).

(2) Bowing *(ruku)*, with the hands placed just above the knees (Photo 4).

(3) Prostrating *(sujud)*, with the forehead and tip of the nose touching the floor, the hands with fingers spread out slightly resting on the floor, and elbows slightly raised (Photo 6).

(4) Sitting *(julus)*, with legs folded under the body (Photo 7).

We will now go over the details of the prayer, using the photos as a guide.

Before beginning the prayer, we ascertain the direction of Ka'aba (*Qibla*), the first house of worship of One God, built by Abraham in Mecca (in what is now Saudi Arabia). This is East, North-East or South-East in the United States and Canada. ● ● ● Placing the covering we have provided on the floor in front of us, we stand straight (Photo 1), facing the direction of Ka'aba (*Qibla*) and silently say that we intend to pray two (or three or four) *rakats* of obligatory (*Fard*) *Fajr* (or *Dhur, 'Asr, Maghrib* or *'Isha*, as the case may be) for the sake of God.

93

••• Now we raise our hands to our face as shown (Photo 2), saying aloud *"Allahu Akbar"* (God is Most Great).

••• We then place our hands wrist over wrist as shown (Photo 3) and silently recite our Praise (*Thana*):

"Subhanaka Allahumma wa bi hamdika,
Glory be to Thee, O God, and Thine is the praise,

wa tabaraka ismuka
and blessed is Thy name,

wa ta'ala jadduka,
and exalted is Thy majesty,

wa la ilaha ghayruka.
and there is none worthy of worship except Thee.

A'udhu Billahi minash shaytanir rajeem."
I take refuge in God from Satan the rejected.

1

2

The last line of this prayer means that we intend in our prayer (*salat*) only to worship God, not to be diverted to other thoughts, and that we seek refuge in God against all temptation.

Remaining in this position, we now recite the opening *surah* (chapter) of Qur'an, *al Fateha*, starting in the name of God. This is recited aloud in the first two *rakats* of *Fajr, Maghrib* and *'Isha* prayer and silently in the first two *rakats* of *Dhur* and *'Asr* prayer, and is always recited silently in the remaining rakats of any prayer.

"Bismillah ar-Rahman ar-Raheem.
In the name of God, the Merciful, the Mercy-Giving.

94

Al-hamdu lillahi Rabbil 'aalamin,
All praise is due to God, Sustainer of the worlds,

ar-Rahman ar-Raheem,
the Merciful, the Mercy-Giving,

Maliki Yawmid Din.
Master of the Day of Judgment.

Iyyaka na'nbudu wa iyyaka nasta'-een.
Thee alone do we worship and from Thee alone do we ask help.

Ihdinas siratal mustaqim,
Show us the straight path,

siratal ladheena an'amta 'alayhim,
the path of those upon whom is Thy favor,

ghayril maghdoobi alayhim,
who have not deserved Thy anger,

wa lad dallin. Ameen."
and who have not gone astray. Amen.

••• Now, in the same posture (Photo 3), we recite a short passage or one of the short *surahs* (chapters) from Qur'an. Some of these short *surahs*, which can be easily memorized, will be found in the Appendix at the end of this booklet.

••• Now we bow with our hands just above our knees as shown (Photo 4), and again say aloud *"Allahu Akbar"* (God is Most Great), and then, in this position, we say silently three times *"Subhana Rabbiyal Adhim"* (Glory be to my Lord, the Almighty).

3

4

••• We then stand erect for a moment as shown (Photo 5) and say aloud once *"Sam'i Allahu liman hamidah"* (God hears those who call upon Him), and then silently once *"Rabbana lakal hamd"* (Our Lord, praise be to Thee).

••• Saying aloud *"Allahu Akbar"* (God is Most Great), we now

95

prostrate as shown (Photo 6) and in this position say silently three times *"Subhana Rabbiyal A'ala"* (Glory be to my Lord, the Most High).

●●● Saying aloud *"Allahu Akbar,"* we lift ourselves to a sitting posture as shown (Photo 7) for a moment's rest before the next prostration, and again saying aloud *"Allahu Akbar,"* we again prostrate as in Photo 6 and again say silently three times *"Subhana Rabbiyal A'ala"* (Glory be to my Lord, the Most High).

| 5 | 6 | 7 |

This completes one unit (*rakat*) of the prayer.

The second *rakat* will be exactly like the first except that after the second prostration, we will again assume the sitting posture of Photo 7 and silently say our Declaration (*Tashahud*):

"At tahiyyatu lillahi was salawatu wat tayyibatu.	All service, all worship and all sanctity are for God.
Assalamu 'alaika ayyuhan nabi, wa rahmatul Lahi wa barakatuhu.	Peace be upon you, O Prophet, and God's mercy and blessings.
Assalamu 'alayna wa 'ala ibadil lahis saliheen.	Peace be upon us and upon those who practice righteousness.
Ashhadu an la ilaha Illahllah,	I bear witness that there is no deity but God, and I bear witness that
wa ashhadu anna Muhammadan abduhu wa rasuluhu."	Muhammad is His servant and messenger.

If this is a two-*rakat* prayer (*Fajr*), we will say in addition here the prayer known as *Salatul Ibraheemiyah* (Ibraheemi Prayer, referring to Abraham).

96

<table>
<tr><td>

"Allahumma salle 'ala Muhammadin wa 'ala ale Muhammad

kama sallayta 'ala Ibraheem wa 'ala ale Ibraheem,

wa barik 'ala Muhammadin wa 'ala ale Muhammad

kama barakta 'ala Ibraheema wa 'ala ale Ibraheem.

Innaka Hameedum Majeed."

</td><td>

O God, exalt Muhammad and the family of Muhammad

as Thou hast exalted Abraham and the family of Abraham,

and bless Muhammad and the family of Muhammad

as Thou hast blessed Abraham and the family of Abraham.

Thou art the Praised, the Glorious.

</td></tr>
</table>

••• In a two-*rakat* prayer, after we have finished this recitation, we turn our faces as shown (Photo 8), first to the right side, saying *"Assalamu alaikum wa rahmatullah"* (Peace be upon you and God's blessings) and then ••• we turn our faces to the left side as shown (Photo 9), saying again *"Assalamu alaikum wa rahmatullah"*

This completes a two-*rakat* prayer, i.e., *Fajr.*

The remaining four prayers of the day have four (*Dhur*), four (*'Asr*), three (*Maghrib*) and four (*'Isha*) *rakats* respectively.

For the three *rakats* of *Maghrib*, we will recite the preceding, saying aloud *Al Fateha* (the oepning *surah* of Qur'an) and an additional short passage from Qur'an which follows it, through the Declaration (*Tashahud*), to complete the first two *rakats*. For the third *rakat*, we will stand again, saying *"Allahu Akbar,"* and silently recite *Al Fateha.* (There is no additional recitation from Qur'an in any *Fard* prayer after the first two *rakats.)* Then we will silently repeat the words and motions of bowing and prostrating for the third *rakat*, which are the same as for the first two *rakats*, and after the second prostration we will say the the Declaration

8

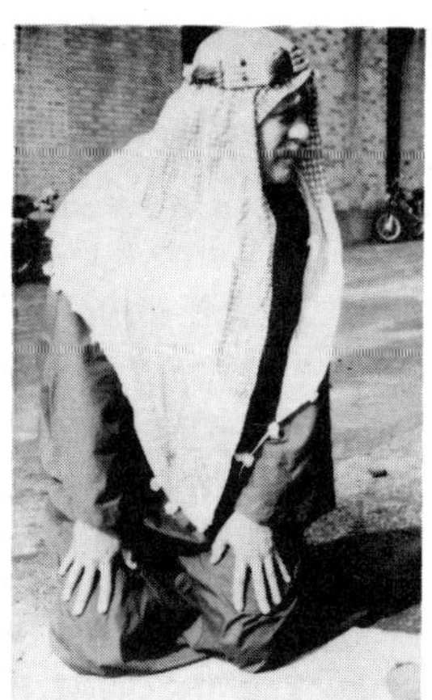

9

97

(*Tashahud*), followed by the Ibrahimi prayer, silently, and end with *"Assalamu alaikum wa rahmatullah"* to each side, aloud.

The four *rakats* of *Dhur*, *'Asr* and *'Isha* are identical, except that the first two *rakats* of *Dhur* and *'Asr* are said silently, while the first two *rakats* of *'Isha* are said aloud, and the last two *rakats* of these four-*rakat* prayers are always said silently. For these prayers, we will say the first two *rakats* as just described, followed by the third and fourth *rakats* which are identical to the first two, except that they are silent. In the fourth *rakat* we sit after the second prostration, silently saying the Declaration (*Tashahud*) followed by the Ibrahimi prayer and ending with *"Assalamu alaikum wa rahmatullah,"* to each side.

This completes the sequence of the required prayers. While it is not difficult to learn this sequence from what has been written here, attending Muslim congregational prayers or asking a Muslim acquaintance to assist in smoothing out this sequence and also in the pronunciation of Arabic will be helpful.

6. SUPEREROGATORY OR ADDITIONAL (SUNNAH) PRAYERS

It was the practice of the Prophet (peace be on him) often to say additional prayers immediately preceding and/or following the prescribed prayers which we have just described. The prescribed prayers are called *Fard* and the additional prayers are called *Sunnah* prayers. The sequence is as follows:

Fajr: 2 *rakats Sunnah* (additional) preceding two *rakats Fard* (prescribed).

Dhur: 2 or 4 *rakats Sunnah* preceding 4 *rakats Fard*, followed by 2 *rakats Sunnah*.

'Asr: no *Sunnah* prayers, or 2 or 4 *rakats Sunnah* preceding 4 *rakats Fard*.

Maghrib: 3 *rakats Fard*, followed by 2 *rakats Sunnah*.

'Isha: 4 *rakats Fard*, followed by 2 complete *rakats Sunnah* followed by 3 *rakats Sunnah*.

7. PERSONAL PRAYER OR SUPPLICATION (DU'A)

Upon the completion of the required (*Fard*) prayers or the *Sunnah* prayers if they are said, we find time and opportunity tó pray to God in our own words (*du'a*) if we wish, expressing whatever is in our hearts, whether it be praise, thanksgiving, asking for forgiveness, supplication for ourselves or for others, or any other thing. This is said sitting, immediately after the formal prayer (*salat*) is over, with the hands held up next to each other, palms up and fingers slightly curled. However, this is optional, not a required or essential part of any prayer. It should be borne in mind that in Islam there is no limit on how often or how much one prays personal prayer (*du'a*) apart from the regular prayers (*salat*) five times each day.

8. UNUSUAL CIRCUMSTANCES

There are many circumstances in which it is not possible to observe prayers in exactly the manner described here. If one is sick, for instance, one can make dry cleansing (*tayammum*) instead of ablution with water (*wudu*) and can pray the entire prayer sitting in the described sitting posture, moving the hands at the proper times to follow the motions, or one can sit instead of standing and bowing but then can perform the prostrations from the sitting posture. If necessary, one can pray lying in bed. When traveling, it is desirable to stop for prayers if possible, but if it is difficult or impossible, one can pray just as one is sitting in the bus, train, plane, etc., moving the hands as usual to follow the motions. In addition, permission is given in Qur'an to shorten the prayers, while traveling, to two *rakats* for each prayer.

It is permitted to combine prayers if it is not possible to observe one prayer at the proper time. *Dhur* may be combined with *'Asr* and *Maghrib* with *'Isha* if necessary. This means that we would first say the four *rakats* of *Dhur*, followed immediately by making a second intention and praying the four *rakats* of *'Asr*, at some time within the time period of *Dhur* and *'Asr*, and the same sequence applies for combining *Maghrib* and *'Isha*. This is appropriate only when we truly are not able to observe some prayer within the proper time limits, but not as a way to avoid the obligation of prayer at regular times five times each day. However, it is our obligation to make up later for any prayer which is not observed at the proper time, whatever the reasons.

99

9. CONGREGATIONAL PRAYERS

It is recommended that when two or more Muslims are present at the time of a prayer they form a congregation and pray together. A leader (*imam*) is selected from among the men in the group, preferably a person of religious knowledge and piety. The leader stands in front by himself, while the rest of the group form straight parallel rows behind him, standing shoulder to shoulder but not touching each other, all facing *Qibla* (the direction of Ka'aba). Women form separate parallel rows behind the men. The whole prayer is performed in the same manner as any individual prayer, with the worshippers following the leader (*imam*) in his movements without preceding him in any act (Photos 10 and 11).

10

11
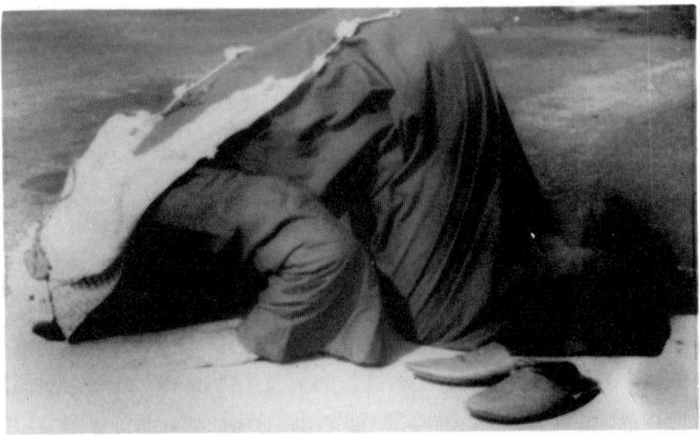

10. THE CALL TO PRAYERS (ADHAN)

If one is praying individually, the call to prayers (*adhan*) is not necessary, although one may give it if he wishes. But for a congregational prayer, *adhan* is given so that the Muslims may know that it is prayer time and assemble at the place of worship. The caller (*muezzin*) stands facing *Qibla* (the direction of Mecca) and with his hands raised to his ears chants in a loud voice.

"Allahu Akbar, Allahu Akbar, Allahu Akbar, Allahu Akbar.	God is Most Great, God is Most Great, God is Most Great, God is Most Great.
Ashhadu an la ilaha Illalah, ashhadu an la ilaha Illahllah	I bear witness that there is no deity but God, I bear witness that there is no deity but God.
Ashhadu anna Muhammadar rasul Allah, ashhadu anna Muhamdar rasul Allah.	I bear witness that Muhammad is a messenger of God, I bear witness that Muhammad is a messenger of God.
Hayya 'alas salah, hayya 'alas salah.	Come to prayer, come to prayer.
Hayya 'alal falah, hayya 'alal falah.	Come to your good, come to your good.
Allahu Akbar, Allahu Akbar.	God is Most Great, God is Most Great.
La ilaha Illallah.	There is no deity but God.

When the *adhan* is given for *Fajr* (dawn) prayer, the following sentence is inserted between the fifth and sixth lines.

"Assalatu khayrum minan nawm, assalatu khayrum minan nawm."	Prayer is better than sleep, prayer is better than sleep.

After *adhan* is called, the worshippers gather at the place of prayer, and when they are assembled, a second call, known as *iqamah* (summons), is recited by one of the congregation. This is identical to the *adhan*, except that it is recited faster and not as loudly, and the following sentence is added between the fifth and sixth lines:

"Qad qammatis salah, qad qammatis salah."	Stand for prayers, stand for prayers.

11. FRIDAY (JUM'A) PRAYER

Apart from the five daily prayers, the Friday (*Jum'a*) congregational prayer is obligatory upon Muslim men and boys. Women, due to their household responsibilities, are excused from the obligation of praying *Jum'a* prayer in congregation and can pray *Dhur* prayer at home as usual. However, if it is possible and convenient, they may join in the congregational *Jum'a* prayer. *Jum'a* prayer consists of two *rakats*, substituting for the four *rakats* of *Dhur*, preceded by a sermon (*khutba*), and is observed at *Dhur* time on Friday, always in congregation. In Muslim countries, Friday (*Jum'a*) is the day of collective worship, and in many places businesses are closed during the prayer time. The Qur'an says about *Jum'a* prayer:

"O you who believe! when the call is proclaimed to prayer on Friday (the Day of Assembly), hasten earnestly to the remembrance of God, and leave off business (and traffic); that is best for you if you but knew. And when the prayer is finished, then you may disperse through the land and seek the bounty of God, and celebrate the praises of God often (and without stint), that you may prosper. But when they see some bargain or some amusement, they disperse headlong to it, and leave thee [the Prophet] standing. Say: the (blessing) from the Presence of God is better than any amusement or bargain. And God is the Best to provide (for all needs)." (62:9-11)

12. EID PRAYER

Eid means a recurring happiness or festivity. There are two *Eids*. The first is called *Eid-ul-Fitr* (The Festival of Fast-Breaking), and it falls on the first day of Shawwal, the tenth month of the Islamic lunar calendar, following the month of Ramadan, in which the revelation of Qur'an was begun and which is the month of fasting. The second *Eid* is *Eid-ul-Adha* (The Festival of Sacrifice), and it falls on the tenth day of Dhul-Hijjah, the last month of the Islamic calendar, following the completion of the course of Pilgrimage (*Hajj*) to Mecca.

The time of the *Eid* prayer is any time after sunrise and before noon on either of the two *Eids*. No call to prayer (*adhan*) or summons (*iqamah*) is required. This prayer consists of two *rakats* with six to sixteen additional *takbirs* *("Allahu Akbar")* offered in congregagation and followed by a sermon (*khutba*).

13. RAMADAN (TARAWIH) PRAYERS

These are prayers offered only during the month of Ramadan, following *'Isha* (night) prayer. They consist of eight to twenty *rakats* offered two by two, with a short break between each two *rakats*, said either alone or preferably in congregation. These prayers are *Sunnah* (additional, supererogatory).

14. FUNERAL (JANAZAH) PRAYER

Prayers to God for a deceased Muslim are a common obligation (*Fard-e Kifayah*) on Muslims. The funeral prayer is offered in congregation and does not have any bowing (*ruku*) or prostration (*sujud*). It consists of four *takbirs* (*"Allahu Akbar"*). Praise (*Thana*) and the opening *surah* (*Al Fateha*) are recited after the first *takbir*, the Ibrahimi prayer after the second *takbir*, the prayer for the dead, for oneself and others in any suitable words one knows, said silently, after the third *takbir*, and the peace greetings (*"Assalamu alaikum wa rahmatullah"*) after the fourth *takbir*.

15. APPENDIX

Some short *surahs* from Qur'an and their translations, suitable for recitation after *Al Fateha* in the first two *rakats* of any prayer, are given here.

SURAT-AL IKHLAS or Purity of Faith (Surah 112)

"Bismillah ar-Rahman ar-Raheem. — In the name of God, the Merciful, the Mercy-giving.

Qul hu Wallaho Ahad, — Say: He is God, the One and Only, God, the Self-sufficient [upon

Allah hus Samad, — Whom everything depends].

Lam yalid wa lam yulad, — He begets not, nor is He begotten,

wa lam yakun lahu kufuwan ahad." — and there is nothing which can be compared to Him.

SURAT-AL NASR or Help (Surah 110)

"Bismillah ar-Rahman ar-Raheem. — In the name of God, the Merciful, the Mercy-giving.

Idha jaa Nasrullahi wal fathu — When comes the help of God, and victory.

wa raayetan nasa yadkhuloona fee deen illahay afwaja, — and thou [the Prophet] seest people enter God's religion in crowds,

fa sabbih bihamdi rabbika — then celebrate the praises of thy Lord

wastagh firhu innahu kana tawwaba." — and pray for His forgiveness, for He is oft-returning (in grace and mercy).

SURAT-AL 'ASR or Time (Surah 103)

"Bismillah ar-Rahman ar-Raheem. — In the name of God, the Merciful the Mercy-giving.

Wal 'asr, — By time

innal insana lafee khusr, — verily man is in loss,

illal ladheena aamanu wa 'amilus salihat, — except such as have faith and do righteous deeds,

wa tawasow bil haqqi wa tawasow bis sabr." — and who counsel each other of truth, and who counsel each other of patience.

"Bismillah ar-Rahman ar-Raheem.

In the name of God, the Merciful, the Mercy-giving.

Iqra be-isme Rabbikal ladhee khalaq,

Read [or Proclaim], in the name of thy Lord Who created,

khalaqal insana min alaq.
created man from a clot.

Iqra wa Rabbukal Akram,
Read [or Proclaim], for thy Lord is Most Bountiful,

al ladhi allama bil qalam -
He Who taught (the use of) the pen -

allamal insana ma lam ya'lam."
taught man that which he knew not.

FASTING

1. INTRODUCTION

Fasting is one of the Five Pillars of Islam. These Five Pillars are:

1. The declaration of faith (*Shahadah*) that there is none worthy of worship and submission except God and that Muhammad is a messenger of God: *"La ilaha illa Allah Muhammadar rasul Allah."*

2. The five daily prayers (*Salat*).

3. Fasting (*Siyam*) every day during the month of Ramadan.

4. The poor-due (*Zakat*), to be given once a year as an obligatory contribution for supporting the poor and needy and other deserving beneficiaries in the community, and

5. Pilgrimage (*Hajj*) to Ka'aba once in one's lifetime if one is physically and financially able.

Although in Islam every act is considered an act of worship if it is done in a lawful manner in order to please God, nevertheless these specific acts of worship, which are the "Pillars" of Islam, are on a higher plane of spirituality. Here we will discuss briefly the spiritual and moral significance of fasting (*Siyam*).

The declaration of faith (*Shahadah*) makes us conscious of the Unity and Sovereignity of God and man's relationship to Him. It frees man from servitude to other human beings and to his own desires, and makes him conscious of the presence of Almighty God and of his responsibilities toward Him. The declaration of faith in the messengership of Muhammad (peace be on him) obliges us to follow the teaching and example of the Prophet in all spheres of life. Through daily prayers (*Salat*), we strengthen our bond with God, develop love for Him, and express our feelings of adoration for His Mercy, Power, Glory and Sovereignty. Through the poor-due

(*Zakat*), we share our wealth with our fellow men for the love of God, without seeking any return, even of gratitude, from them. This develops a spirit of generosity and brotherhood in us and makes us conscious that we enjoy wealth and property through the bounty of Him to Whom everything really belongs. The pilgrimage (*Hajj*) purifies us from all kinds of prides and prejudices, makes us aware that national, racial and social differences have no significance in the sight of God, and that only true faith, like that of Abraham (peace be on him), and righteousness are the essence of man's worth.

Returning again to the subject of fasting (*Siyam*), we remark that fasting is an act of pure submission to God's command, given in the Qur'an, to observe the fast. Fasting has many benefits, which we will discuss presently, but its true significance is to develop a sense of complete obedience to the One Who created us and gave us our physical and spiritual needs and the means to fulfill these needs. We acknowledge that God is our Sustainer, and through His bounty — through the use of natural resources and our faculties — we obtain our sustenance. Hence, if God commands us to abstain from food, drink and the fulfillment of other natural appetites for a period of time, we gladly obey His command. God says in Qur'an:

> "O you who believe! Fasting is ordained for you as it was ordained for those before you, so that you may remain conscious of God." (2:183)

While many benefits come to us through fasting the primary benefit is that we learn self-restraint, discipline of our appetites, and flexibility of our habits. Over-indulgence in eating, drinking, smoking or marital relations makes one the slave of his desires and habits. Through fasting one becomes free of this slavery. Through fasting those who are well-off learn to appreciate the afflictions of the poor — hunger and thirst — and become more sympathetic toward them. When a person fasts, he feels that he is joining the whole Muslim world in a spiritual act, thus increasing his sense of community and brotherhood. Some benefits to a person's health also result from fasting, such as the elimination of fatty substances from the blood, a decrease in the harmful activity of intestinal microbes and of uric acid, and so on. But it should be emphasized that all these benefits are not the object of fasting.

107

As was stated earlier, we fast solely because God commands us to do so, as devout and obedient servants to His will.

Prophet Muhammad (peace be on him) is reported to have said:

"He who fasts during Ramadan with faith and seeking reward from God will have his past sins forgiven."

"Fasting is a shield (against acts of disobedience in this world and against the fire in the next)."

2. RAMADAN — THE MONTH OF FASTING

Ramadan is the ninth month of the Islamic calendar, which is based on the orbiting of the moon (lunar calendar) rather than on the orbiting of the earth (solar calendar). We will comment on this a little later. Here we will discuss the significance of the month of Ramadan, chosen by God for Muslims as the month of fasting. Almighty God says in Qur'an:

"It was in the month of Ramadan in which the Qur'an was (first) revealed as guidance unto man and a self-evident proof of that guidance, and as the standard by which to discern the true from the false. Hence, whoever of you is present (at home) shall fast throughout it." (2:185)

Thus, Ramadan is the month in which every single day is a day of fasting.

3. THE NIGHT OF POWER (LAILAT-UL-QADR)

The night in which Prophet Muhammad (peace be on him) first received the Divine message through the agency of the Angel Gabriel is referred to in the Qur'an as "The Night of Power" (*Lailat-ul-Qadr*). It is not known exactly which night of Ramadan is the Night of Power, but according to sound traditions of the Prophet (*Hadith*), it is one of the odd-numbered nights of the last ten days of Ramadan. In some Muslim countries the night preceding the twenty-seventh day of Ramadan is observed as the Night of Power, but one cannot be sure about this date. In Qur'an it is said about this Night:

"We have indeed revealed this (Qur'an) in the Night of Power. And what would explain to thee the significance of the Night of Power? The Night of Power is better than a thousand months. Therein descend the angels and the Spirit [Gabriel] by God's

permission, on every errand.   Peace — until the day breaks."
(97:1-5)

The Holy Prophet (peace be on him) is reported to have said: "When the Night of Power comes, Gabriel descends with a company of angels who invoke blessings on everyone who is standing or sitting and remembering the Most Great and Glorious God."

'Aisha, the Prophet's wife, said that God's messenger Muhammad (peace be on him) used to exert himself in devotion during the last ten nights of Ramadan to a greater extent than at any other time.

4. THE BATTLE OF BADR

An event of great historical importance for Muslims took place during Ramadan. The Battle of Badr was fought on the 17th of Ramadan in the year 2 A.H. (After *Hijra*). It marked the first open struggle between the newly-organized Islamic community in Medina and the enemies of Islam, the pagans of Mecca. The Muslims were outnumbered three to one, were poorly equipped and inexperienced in warfare, but under the inspiring leadership of the Prophet (peace be on him) they fought with couraged and valor, and God granted them victory.

5. THE ISLAMIC LUNAR CALENDAR

It may be noted that all religious observances in Islam are based on the lunar rather than the solar calendar, and there is a significance in this. For example, let us consider Ramadan. Since the lunar year consists of 354 days, it is eleven days (twelve days in a leap year) shorter than the solar year. The month of Ramadan thus rotates gradually through all the seasons — winter, fall, summer and spring. In winter the days are short and cold and fasting is easiest, while in summer the long, hot days make fasting more difficult, and fall and spring bring an intermediate situation. Thus Muslims, whether they live in the Northern or the Southern Hemisphere, become accustomed to fasting in all seasons, sometimes with greater ease and sometimes with greater hardship. If, however, the period of fasting had been fixed in a particular season — say winter in the Northern Hemisphere while it was summer in the Southern Hemisphere — it would have resulted in perpetual ease for one group of Muslims, while the other group suffered perpetual hardship.

Furthermore, a new moon can be sighted by a nomad in the desert and a settler in the town alike, by one who can read calendars and by one who is totally illiterate, and no precise knowledge of the reckoning of dates and days is necessary. In addition, the sighting of the new moon, especially that of Ramadan and that of Eid, provides great excitement in itself.

6. KINDS OF FASTING

A. Obligatory

Fasting in Ramadan is obligatory (*fard*) on every Muslim man and woman, with a few exceptions to be mentioned later. Any day of Ramadan on which one does not fast should be made up on a later date.

B. Supererogatory (Additional)

This includes fasts on specific days of the year, such as any six days of Shawwal, the 9th, 10th and 11th of Muharram, the 15th of Shaban, etc. These were recommended and practiced by the Prophet (*sunnah*) but are not obligatory.

C. Optional

These include all voluntary fasts. It should be borne in mind that the Prophet (peace be on him) asked Muslims not to fast for long periods, saying "You have duties to fulfill even with regard to yourself."

D. Forbidden

Prophet Muhammad (peace be on him) forbade fasting on the two *Eids, Eid-ul-Fitr* (the Festival of Fast Breaking) and *Eid-ul-Adha* (the Festival of Sacrifice), and on the three days following *Eid-ul-Adha*. All these are days of thanksgiving, joy and happiness, while fasting involves hardship.

7. KEEPING THE FAST

The period of keeping fast is from before dawn (about two

hours before sunrise) until sunset. During this period, one may not eat, drink or smoke, and married people in addition may not have marital relations. In addition, chewing or swallowing anything external or taking medicine through the mouth or nose is not permitted.

Eating, drinking or putting something in the mouth *unintentionally* (i.e., forgetting that you are fasting), use of perfume, ointments or skin creams, external medications, brushing the teeth or rinsing the mouth, swallowing saliva, washing one's body, does not break the fast.

However, eating, drinking, smoking or breaking the fast in any other manner *deliberately, without valid reason* (i.e., sickness, travel or the onset of menstruation), is an act of breaking one's commitment or intention to fast on a particular day (see below), and it carries a heavy penalty: eithei to feed sixty people the equivalent of one meal each, or to give the equivalent amount to sixty people in charity, or to fast for sixty days to make up for that one day's broken fast. On the other hand, if one does not to fast on a given day during Ramadan, whatever be the reasons, this is to be made up later, a day for a day.

8. EVENING MEAL

It is customary to break one's fast as soon as the sun has set with a light snack (often with one or three dates, according to the Prophet's custom). Before one begins to eat, he says, again according to the practice of the Prophet (peace be on him):

"Allahumma, laka sumto, wa bika amanto, wa 'ala rizqika aftarto. Bismillah ar-Rahman ar-Raheem."

O God, I have fasted for You, and I have believed in You, and with Your food I break the fast. In the name of God, the Merciful, the Mercy-giving.

This breaking of the fast is called *iftar*. It is followed by *Maghrib* (sunset) prayer, which may be followed at one's convenience by a full dinner. It is suggested not to overeat in order to compensate for the period of fasting. This is a good time to drink plenty of water or other fluid, which the body needs.

111

9. MORNING MEAL

It is also customary to take another meal during the night, as always beginning with the name of God ("*Bismillah ar-Rahman ar-Raheem*"), resuming the fast at least twenty minutes before dawn begins to break. This meal is called *suhoor*. Any food will be found suitable for this meal, but common sense dictates that highly salted or highly seasoned food should not be taken and that protein foods are helpful in maintaining a high energy level during the day. After the pre-dawn meal is finished, one privately makes the intention of fasting for the day ahead. For example, one may say: "O God, I intend to fast today in obedience to Your command and only to seek Your pleasure." If one wishes, he may spend the interval between the end of eating until dawn in reading Qur'an or any other Islamic reading and as soon as dawn has broken, *Fajr* (dawn) prayer is performed.

10. EXEMPTIONS FROM FASTING

The following people are exempt from fasting:

A. Sick people whose health is likely to be severely affected by the observance of fasting. They may postpone the fast as long as they are sick and make up for it later, a day for a day.

B. People who are travelling (i.e., they have left their homes and are on the road, or when reaching their destination they have the intention of returning in a few days). Such people may not fast temporarily during their travel days only. They are to make up later the days which were missed, a day for a day. But it is better for them, as Qur'an points out, to observe the fast during their travels if they can do so without extraordinary hardship.

C. Pregnant women and nursing mothers may also not keep the fast, but they must make up for it later, a day for a day.

D. Women during the period of menstruation (maximum of ten days) or of confinement after childbirth (maximum of forty days) should not fast. They must postpone the fast until these periods are over and then make up for it, a day for a day.

E.   Men and women who are too old and feeble to undertake the obligation and to bear its hardships. Such people are exempt from this duty, but if they can afford it, they must offer to at least one needy Muslim an average full meal (or its value) for each day of Ramadan on which they have not fasted. Whenever they are able to fast, even if it is for only one day of the month, they should do so and should compensate for the remainder.

F.   Children under the age of puberty are exempt from the obligation of fasting. However, before they reach the age at which fasting becomes an obligation, it is good to encourage them to fast for a few days during Ramadan.

G.   Insane persons are exempt from the obligation of fasting.

11. TARAWIH PRAYERS

These are supererogatory (additional, optional) prayers performed during the month of Ramadan after the fifth prayer of the day, *'Isha* (night) prayer. These prayers consist of eight, ten or twenty units (*rakats*), each two or four units (*rakats*) completing one cycle of the prayers. These prayers are not obligatory but are highly recommended, according to the Prophet's own practice (*sunnah*), especially during the last ten days of Ramadan.

12. ZAKAT-UL-FITR OR SADAQAT-UL-FITR

It is the religious duty of all Muslims to see that the poor in the community are not left uncared for. With this in view, Islam requires that all persons who can afford it should give a contribution to the poor any time before *Eid* day or on *Eid* day before the *Eid* prayer begins. This charity is known as *zakat-ul-fitr* or *sadaqat-ul-fitr*. The Holy Prophet (peace be on him) is reported to have said: "Fasting during Ramadan is not acceptable to God without *sadaqat-ul-fitr*" and "*Sadaqat-ul-fitr* is a means of purification of one who is fasting." This amount should be equivalent to at least one meal (roughly one dollar in the United States per person in a family.

113

13. RECOMMENDATIONS DURING RAMADAN

Since Ramadan is a month of spiritual discipline, it is recommended that one should go beyond the regular prayers and fasting. Besides *Tarawih* prayers, other things are recommended.

A. Reading the Holy Qur'an:

One should try to complete the reading of Qur'an from beginning to end at least once during Ramadan. Needless to say, prayers should be observed with absolute regularity.

B. Giving charity:

One of the functions of fasting is to make Muslims realize how it feels to be hungry, i.e., needy. Giving charity is therefore quite closely related to fasting and it should be given to the fullest extent one can afford.

C. Paying the obligatory Zakat (poor-due):

Zakat is the Fourth Pillar of Islam. It is recommended that one should pay his annual *zakat* every Ramadan. Muslims in this country who do not know of any persons eligible to receive *zakat* may send the money to the Muslim Students' Association of U.S. and Canada for distribution to the deserving, as mentioned in Qur'an 9:61.

D. Restraining the temper, refraining from gossip and back-biting, and the doing of whatever is good are desirable at all times, but especially during Ramadan. Fasting and becoming angry or speaking ill of others do not go hand-in-hand.

14. EID-UL-FITR

After Ramadan, the month of fasting, has ended, *Eid-ul-Fitr* — the Festival of Fast Breaking — takes place on the first day of the succeeding month, Shawwal. *Eid* is a day of thanksgiving and rejoicing for the fulfillment of the obligation of fasting according to God's command. In the morning, at some time after sunrise and before midday, a special congregational prayer consisting of two units (*rakats*), with sixt to sixteen additional *takbirs* (recitations of "*Allahu Akbar*" [God is Most Great]), is offered, followed by a sermon (*khutba*) by the leader of the prayer (the *imam*). A period of marked joy and happiness follows the prayers. The Holy Prophet (peace be on him) has said: "A fasting person will have joy and happiness twice: when he breaks the fast [i.e., he will be full of joy because of breaking the fast], and when he meets his Lord on the Day of Judgment [he will be full of joy because he had kept his obligation of fasting] ."

Sowm (singular)
Siyam (plural) = fast. In Islam a fast starts before dawn and ends at sunset. There is no fasting during the night.

Ramadan = the ninth month of the Islamic (lunar) calendar. Each day of Ramadan is a day of fasting.

Suhur = pre-dawn meal on a day of fasting.

Iftar = breaking of the fast at sunset with food or drink.

Lailat-ul-Qadr = the Night of Power. One of the odd-numbered night in the last ten days of Ramadan during which the first revelation of the Holy Qur'an came to Prophet Muhammad (peace be on him).

Eid-ul-Fitr = the Festival of Fast-Breaking. The day of celebration and thanksgiving after the end of Ramadan. It takes place on the first day of Shawwal, the tenth month of the Islamic (lunar) calendar.

Zakat-ul-Fitr or **Sadaqat-ul-Fitr** = the obligatory alms, equivalent to the price of one meal, to be given to the poor or needy some time before Eid day or on Eid day itself before the Eid prayer.

1. THE MEANING OF ZAKAT AND ITS IMPORTANCE

Zakat is the Fourth Pillar of Islam. It is an obligation *(fard)*, prescribed by God on those Muslim men and women who possess enough means, to distribute a certain percentage of their annual savings or capital in goods or money among the poor and the needy. *Zakat* is assessed at the end of the year on both capital and savings from income. The details of percentages and the method of distribution and collection are based on the practices of Prophet Muhammad (peace be on him) and his Companions, and will be discussed in a later section of this unit

The literal meaning of the word *zakat* is 'purity'. The The Prophet (peace be on him) has said: "God has made *zakat* obligatory simply to purify your remaining property." There is no equivalent practice in other religions. Hence, while terms such as 'charity,' poor-tax', 'alms-tax' and 'poor-due' have been coined by various translators, none of these terms actually conveys the true sense of the word *zakat*. *Zakat* is not a tax levied by a government, nor is it a voluntary contribution. It is first and foremost a duty enjoined by God and hence a form of worship. In Qur'an the payment of *zakat* is frequently mentioned in the same sentence or verse as the establishment of *salat* (prayers).

"Lo! Those who believe and do good deeds and establish *salat* and pay *zakat*, their reward is with their Sustainer; and no fear shall come upon them, nor shall they grieve." (2:277)

"These are verses of the Book full of wisdom, a guide and mercy to the doers of good — those who establish *salat* and pay *zakat* and have the assurance of the Hereafter. These are on guidance from their Sustainer, and these are the ones who will prosper."

(31:1-5)

Thus, while *salat* is an act of worship through words and bodily action, *zakat* is a devotional act through one's wealth. Without the spirit of submission to God and love of Him, both acts are without spiritual and moral significance.

From a practical point of view, it is the duty of an Islamic state to collect *zakat* from every Muslim who meets the requirements for paying it. The first Caliph, Abu Bakr Siddiq, declared war on those tribes which refused to pay *zakat* while still professing Islam and observing daily prayers. He reasoned that the Divine law (*Shari'ah*) cannot be divided and that one cannot follow part of the Holy Book and cast aside other parts. However, in a non-Islamic state it is up to the individual Muslim to be conscientious enough to voluntarily fulfill this duty to God and to his community, and it is up to his brother Muslims to remind him of this duty.

2. THE SPIRIT OF ZAKAT

In the Holy Qur'an, wealth is referred to as God's bounty (*fadl*). God, as the Creator and Sustainer of the universe, is also the Owner of all things, including all the things which man possesses and uses.

"Who has created the heavens and the earth and sends down rain for you from the sky? With it We caused to grow orchards full of loveliness; it is not in your power to make trees grow in them."

(27:60)

Since God is the true Owner of all things and we are merely His trustees, wealth is to be produced, distributed, acquired and spent in a way which is pleasing to Him. The acquisition of wealth is not an end in itself, nor is wealth to be squandered for meaningless or wasteful purposes, and above all it is not to be used in order to gain power over other people through exploitation or control of the means of livelihood. Qur'an and *Hadith* make it very clear that any form of gain which results in some injustice or harm to others is an act of disobedience to God. On the other hand, Qur'an tells us that next to purity of faith, the most pleasing thing in the sight of God is kindness and charity, forbearance and forgiveness, and doing good to others.

"Those who spend in charity, whether in prosperity or adversity, who restrain anger and pardon people; for God loves those who do good to others." (3:134)

Thus, God enjoins on us humility before the Creator and His creatures, moderation in the satisfaction of our legitimate needs and desires, control of our appetites, and a spirit of generosity and charity, while He asks us to shun pride in ourselves and contempt for others, self-indulgence and pleasure-seeking, and greed for material things and worldly power. We

find, therefore, that prayers (*salat*) are made obligatory to pur
ify our hearts from every kind of pride, fasting (*seeyam*) tc
control our appetites, and *zakat* to overcome greed. The spirit
behind all these acts of worship ought to be the spirit of submission to God, gratitude for all His bounties, and hope for His
forgiveness and mercy.

In particular, it is with utmost gratitude and joy that a
Muslim who possesses enough means that *zakat* is obligatory for
him should fulfill his obligation — gratitude for the bounties
which God has showered upon him and joy in being able to
help others. Because the payment of *zakat* is a duty to God,
no one should ever think of it as a favor done to the person who
receives it. In fact, it is his right to receive it and the obligation of the giver to give it. Like any other act of worship in
Islam, in giving *zakat* it is necessary that the intention of the
giver and receiver be pure and honest.

3. THE BENEFITS OF ZAKAT

The moral and material benefits of *zakat* are obvious
Giving *zakat* purifies the heart of the giver from selfishness anc
greed for wealth and develops in him sympathy for the poor anc
needy. And receiving *zakat* purifies the heart of the recipien
from envy and hatred of the rich and prosperous, and fosters ir
him a sense of good will toward his brother Muslims who
although they are better off, have shared their wealth witl
him for the sake of God.

God syas in Qur'an:

"To Him belong the keys of the heavens and earth; He enlarges
or restricts the sustenance to whom He wills, for He knows full well
all things." (42:12)

"He has raised some of you in ranks above others that He may try
you in the gifts He has given you." (6:165)

Thus, a Muslim, whether prosperous or needy, considers his
condition in this world as a test from God. Those who have
wealth have the obligation to be generous and charitable and to
share the bounties of God with their brothers, while those who
are poor have the obligation to be patient, to work to improve
their situation, and to be free of envy. Qur'an tells us that it is

not a man's wealth or position but his God-consciousness, the quality of his character, and the manner in which he uses whatever is given to him by God which determines his ultimate destiny in the Hereafter. The Prophet (peace be on him) has said: "The generous man is near God, near Paradise, near men, and far from Hell, but the miserly man is far from God, far from Paradise, far from men, and near Hell. Indeed, an ignorant man who is generous is dearer to God than a worshipper who is miserly."

The economic objective of Islam is just and humane distribution of wealth, as stated in Qur'an:

"...so that this (wealth) may not circulate solely among the rich from among you." (59:7)

Thus, Islam neither approves of hoarding and unlimited building up of capital, nor of compulsory equal distribution of wealth, as both are unjust. Its teaching encourages the earning of a livelihood and acquisition of wealth by lawful, honest and productive means, and enjoins the just sharing of the acquired wealth among the workers, the investors and the community at large. The community's share in the produced wealth is *zakat* and *sadaqah* (charity), the first an obligatory and the second a voluntary contribution from individuals. *Zakat*, when honestly practiced, results in freeing the society from class distinctions, rivalries, suspicion and corruption. It produces a community of people who love and respect each other, and who have sympathy and concern for each other's welfare.

Giving *zakat* is not a matter of pride. It is a devotional act, like *salat*, on the completion of which the contributor should be thankful to God for the fulfilment of his obligation and pray for the forgiveness of his sins.

4. KINDS OF PROPERTY ON WHICH ZAKAT IS OBLIGATORY

Zakat is compulsory on cash, cattle and crops (three c's). The regulations differ for each of these categories. As the detailed system of computation in the last two catagories is rather complicated, it will not be discussed here. Such information is available in standard books on Islamic jurisprudence.

For cash, the minimum rate is two and one-half percent (2½%). *Zakat* should be given only on the net balance after all

120

lawful expenses have been met at the end of the year. The rate mentioned above is only a lower limit. There is no upper limit, except that one should not deprive himself and his dependents from meeting their lawful necessities. Beyond these obligations, the more one gives, the greater the benefit on both the giver and the recipient.

5. RECIPIENTS OF ZAKAT

Those who are eligible to receive *zakat* are mentioned in the Holy Qur'an.

"The alms are only for the poor, the needy, those who collect them, those whose hearts are to be reconciled, to free the captives and the debtors, for the cause of God, and for the travellers; a duty imposed by God. God is All-Knowing, All-Wise." (9:60)

It should be remembered that these categories of persons who are to be helped by *zakat* were laid down fourteen hundred years ago. They are equally applicable to our own time.

1. **The poor**: Those who are unable to work or do not have sufficient means to support themselves and their families, or those who are engaged in the way of God and are unable to earn their livelihood. Those who do not ask are preferable.

2. **The needy**: Those people who, due to some calamity, have lost their possessions should be supported by these funds in order to provide them means for earning a living.

3. **Zakat collectors**: The salaries of these workers may be paid from this fund. According to some authorities, this category refers to the revenue department or even the entire government of an Islamic state or to workers in a public fund.

4. **Converts**: Those people who have embraced Islam and consequently lost all their worldly assets should be helped, and attempts should be made to settle them in a normal life.

5. **People who are not free**: This category would include payment of ransom for freeing Muslim hostages or prisoners of war from their captors.

6. **Debtors**: People who are unable to pay debts incurred due to pressing lawful needs. Those who have incurred debts by extravagance in marriage and other purposes of display of wealth and ostentation cannot claim help from these funds.

7. **Wayfarers and travellers**: Those people who are rendered

helpless in a foreign country due to lawful reasons such as preaching Islam, pursuing an education, business, etc., may be helped under this heading. The money may also be given to welfare organizations which dispense help of this kind.

8. **In the way of God**: This category embaraces general help to the public or to a good cause for which people are striving. Under this heading, money could be utilized as follows:

A.   It could be given to those who can help propagate the massage of Islam;

B.   It could be provided as stipends to students, scholars and researchers;

C.   It could be used in organizing or improving organizations beneficial to the community, for example, hospitals, educational institutions, libraries, mosques, groups working for the service of Islam, and for the propagation of knowledge.

6. SOME REGULATIONS CONCERNING ZAKAT

The legal dependents of the contributor may not receive *zakat* from him.

Money exceeding the recipient's requirements   is not to be given, nor may the recipient accept more than enough to meet his requirements.

Taxes which are paid to the government are not included in the category of *zakat*.

The contributor should not indulge in pride nor seek fame by carrying out this duty, but if the mention of his name is likely to encourage others to pay *zakat*, it is permissible to give his name.

It is not necessary to tell the recipient that he is receiving *zakat* money. If there are deserving persons who will not accept the money if they know it is *zakat*, it can be given without specifying its source. The contributor, however, still gives it as his *zakat* payment.

Zakat may be distributed directly to the individuals or organizations mentioned above. The contributor should use his best possible judgment to find the most deserving beneficiaries. In the past, when there were legally constituted Islamic governments, *zakat* was collected through official channels and its distribution was the function of a special department of the government. In the present day, however, especially in non-Muslim countries, giving *zakat* is an obligation for which each Muslim adult must take responsibility each year himself. In this country, Muslims may give their *zakat* directly to some deserving needy person, of whom there are many in every community, or he may give it for use as *zakat* to some Islamic organization, such as the Muslim Students' Association of United States and Canada, which has a *zakat* fund. Possible suggested uses of the collected *zakat* money on this continent would be in helping our brother Muslims in other countries, in organizing youth camps and training centers for the education of Muslim children growing up here, in helping organizations serving Islam in the United States and Canada, in supporting Muslim educational institutions or hospitals, and in any other efforts for the cause of Islam.

7. SADAQAH (CHARITY)

Zakat is an obligation on Muslim men and women who are better off financially. *Sadaqah* (charity) refers to any other act of charity.

1. **Charity — an essential part of righteousness:** To give to help others from one's possessions, no matter whether they are many or few, is a necessary part of a Muslim's sense of submission to God and his concern for his fellow human beings. God says in Qur'an:

"You shall not attain righteousness unless you spend on others of that which you love, and whatever you spend, verily God has knowledge of it." (3:92)

The Holy Prophet (peace be on him) has said: "Son of Adam! To give away what is beyond your needs is better for you and to withhold it is worse for you, but you are not blamed for having sufficiency. Give first to those who are dependent on you."

2. **What to spend in charity:** God says in Qur'an:

"They ask thee what to spend (in charity). Say: What is beyond your needs." (2:219)

"O you who believe! Spend of the good things which you have earned, and of that which We bring forth from the earth for you,

and do not seek to give the bad things (in charity), when you would
not take them for yourselves except with disdain." (2:267)

The Prophet (peace be on him) exhorted: "Spend; do not calculate and so have God calculating against you; do not hoard and so have God hoarding from you; but give such small amounts as you can."

4. **How to give charity:** The best charity is that which is given in secret, in order to respect the dignity of the recipient and to keep the motives of the giver free of pride or desire for praise. Qur'an says:

"O you who believe! Do not cancel your charity by reminders of your generosity or by injury, like those who spend their substance to be seen men but do not believe either in God or in the Last Day." (2:264)

"Kind words and the covering of faults are better than charity followed by injury. God is free of all wants, and He is most forbearing." (2:263)

The Prophet (peace be on him) has said: "The best charity is that which the right hand gives and the left hand does not know of it."

5. **Recipients of charity:** Charity starts with one's own family and dependents and extends to relatives, to the poor and the needy of the community, to widows and orphans, debtors, travellers, those who strive or who migrate in the cause of God, and finally to any others in need. Qur'an says:

"They ask thee what they should spend (in charity). Say: What ever of your wealth you spend shall be for the parents and for the near of kin and the orphans and the needy and the traveller; and whatever good you do, verily, God has full knowledge of it."
(2:215; also 9:60)

"(Charity is) for those in need, who, in God's cause are restricted (from travel) and cannot move about in the land, seeking (for trade or work). The ignorant man thinks, because of their dignity, that they are free from want. You shall know them by their mark: they do not beg insistently from all and sudry. And whatever of good you give, be assured that God knows it well." (2:273)

Finally, in a broader sense, it is important to stress that the meaning of charity is not confined to money or things given to help someone in need. It includes everything we do or say to help others - our time, our energy, our concern, our sympathy, our attitude of support, our words of kindness, our prayers. To care for the needs of a neighbor, to minister to the wants of a child, to visit the sick, to go the funeral of an acquaintance, to console the bereaved — all these are acts of charity. There are many *hadiths* (saying of the Prophet) which emphasize clearly how broad the meaning of charity is, among which are the following: "When you smile in your brother's face, or enjoin what is reputable, or forbid what is objectionable or direct someone who has lost his way, or help a man who has bad eyesight, or remove stones, thorns and bones from the road, or pour water from your bucket into your brother's, it counts to you as charity," and "Every act of kindness is charity." May God Most High guide each of us to do our utmost, in the true Islamic spirit of brotherhood, in charity.

KEY WORDS AND DEFINITIONS

Mecca = a city in the Arabian peninsula sacred to Muslims because it contains the sacred Ka'aba.

Ka'aba = a simple cubic structure, the Most Ancient House of God, first built by the Prophet Ibrahim and his son the Prophet Ismael (peace be on them).

Qibla = the direction of Ka'aba, which Muslims everywhere face when they pray from any place on earth.

Hajj = the Major Pilgrimage to Mecca during the prescribed months.

'Umra = the Minor Pilgrimage to Mecca, for which there is no specific time.

Hajju at-Tamattu' = the Interrupted Pilgrimage (performing *umra* followed by a short interruption before performing *hajj*).

Ihram = the pilgrim's dress, signifying the state of consecration to God.

Tawaf = going around (Ka'aba).

Sa'ai = hastening (between the two hills of as-Safa and al-Marwa).

Talbiya = devotional calls.

Zamzam = a well in Mecca, first found by the Prophet Ismael (peace be on him) when his mother Hagar was looking for water after being left alone in Mecca.

Al-Hajar ul-Aswad = the Black Stone, a remainder of the original Ka'aba built by the Prophet Ibrahim and the Prophet Ismael (peace be on them).

As-Safa and al-Marwa = two small hills in Mecca.

Arafat = the name of a mountain and a plain near Mecca.

Mina = a town near Mecca.

Dhul-Hijja = the twelfth month of the Islamic (lunar) calendar.

Eid-ul-Adha = the Festival of Sacrifice, occurring on the tenth day of Dhul-Hijja.

Al-Masjid al-Nabawi = the Prophet's Mosque in Medina.

Al-Masjid al-Aqsa = the Farthest Mosque, built on the site of Solomon's Temple in Jerusalem.

Ibrahim = Abraham, a prophet of God (peace be on him).

Hajer = Hagar, wife of the Prophet Ibrahim.

Isma'ail = Ishmael, also a prophet of God, son of the Prophet Ibrahim and Hajer (peace be on them).

In the name of Allah, the Beneficent, the Merciful

1. THE MEANING OF HAJJ

The Arabic word *hajj* means 'to set out for a definite purpose.' Specifically, it refers to the pilgrimage to Ka'aba, which is situated in the city of Mecca in Arabia, and the performance of certain observances (*manasik*) during the months prescribed for *hajj*. The observances of *hajj* are based on the Qur'an (2:196-203, 5:98-100, 22-27:32) and the *Sunnah* (the practice of Prophet Muhammad, peace be on him), and they commemorate certain events in the lives of the Prophet Abraham (Ibrahim), his wife Hagar (Hajer), and their son the Prophet Ishmael (Isma'il) (peace be on them). These observances and their significance will be described later. Here we would like to stress the fact that the main object of *hajj*, as of any other form of Islamic worship, is to create the spirit of submission to God and to nourish spiritual joy. The Holy Prophet has said:

"Those who perform the *hajj* or *'umra* are people who have come to visit God [that is, they have come with the sole intention of worshipping God]. If they supplicate Him, He will respond to them, and if they ask of Him forgiveness, He will forgive them."

2. THE SIGNIFICANCE OF HAJJ

The spirit of *hajj* is the spirit of total sacrifice — of personal comforts, worldly pleasures, the acquisition of wealth, the companionship of relatives and friends, vanities of dress and personal appearance, pride relating to birth, national origin, accomplishments, work or social status. This sacrifice of self was attained to the highest degree by the Prophet Ibrahim (peace be on him), who is known as 'The Friend of God' *(Khalil-ul-Allah)*. The story of his sacrifice is narrated in the Qur'an:

"[Ibrahim said] 'O my Sustainer! Grant me a righteous (son)!'
So We gave him the good news of a boy [Ismael] ready to suffer

128

and forbear. Then, when (the son) reached (the age of serious) work with him, he said, 'O my son! I see in vision that I offer you in sacrifice: now see what is your view.' (The son) said: 'O my father! Do as you are commanded. You will find me, if God so wills, one practicing patience and constancy.' So when they had both sumitted their wills (to God), and he [Ibrahim] had laid him [Ismael] prostrate on his forehead (for sacrifice), We called out to him, 'O Ibrahim! You have already fulfilled the vision!' — thus indeed do We reward those who do right. For this was obviously a trial. And We ransomed him with a great sacrifice. And We left (this blessing) for him among generations (to come) in later times: 'Peace and salutation to Ibrahim!' " (27:100-109)

Although the events to which this narrative refers occurred many centuries ago (roughly 2000 B.C.), they have a very clear and direct meaning for us today, as they did at the time of Prophet Muhammad (peace be on him). The significance of Abraham's willingness to sacrifice his son, who was dearer to him than anything else in the world, at God's command, is a clear demonstration that to him obedience to God was more important than any earthly possession or tie, no matter how precious it might be. The spirit of submission to God cannot be illustrated for us in any clearer manner than this.

The *Hajj* also signifies the brotherhood of all Muslims, which is demonstrated and emphasized in a concrete manner in this greatest of all international assemblies. If the true spirit of *hajj* were carried through into our daily lives, Muslims everywhere could achieve the same oneness and the same unity now known only during *hajj*, for at that time the ordinary distinctions and differences among human beings are erased. During *hajj* Muslims of every race and color and language, of diverse cultures and backgrounds, of various social, economic and educational levels, all respond to the call of God, all dressed in the same simple manner — the two pieces of white, unsewn cloth which constitute the pilgrim's dress — all performing the same actions in the same way for the same single purpose: the glorification of Almighty God. This oneness of physical appearance and singleness of purpose also impresses upon the minds of the pilgrims that all human beings are equal in the sight of God and that all will be accountable to Him. Thus *hajj* also reminds Muslims of the ultimate assembly of the Day of Judgment, when all human beings will stand equal

129

before Almighty God, to receive their reward or punishment.

Hajj also reminds Muslims of the birth, rise and expansion of Islam, the overthrow of idolatry, the establishment of the worship of One God, and the difficulties and achievements of the Holy Prophet Muhammad (peace be on him) and the early Muslims.

3. MECCA

Mecca is the sacred city of Islam, located in the Arabian peninsula. The city lies in a long, irregular valley fringed with low hills and exposed passes. Its climate is extremely hot and dry. Despite its heat and sterility, which make it poorly suited for human habitation, Mecca was in times past the trade and cultural center of Arabia. The historical importance of Mecca is related to the Ka'aba, the Prophet Ibrahim, his son the Prophet Ismael (peace be on them), and their descendants.

Mecca and Medina (situated some 225 miles northwest of Mecca) are the two cities most dear to Muslims because of their great reverence and love for the Holy Prophet Muhammad (peace be on him). The Prophet was born in Mecca and was buried in Medina, and, excepting short periods of travel, spent all his life in these two cities (see Unit 2: Prophet Muhammad).

4. KA'ABA

The word Ka'aba means 'a cube-shaped structure.' It refers in particular to the cube-shaped building in Mecca constructed of stone and mortar, measuring approximately 45 feet in height, 33 feet in width and 50 feet in length, which is generally covered with a black cloth decorated with Qur'anic verses worked in gold. Ka'aba is also known as the Most Ancient House *(Baitul-Atiq)*, the Sacred Mosque *(al-Masjid al-Haram)*, and the House of God *(Baitu-Allah)*. Muslims all over the world face the direction of the Ka'aba when they perform their five daily prayers in accordance with the injunction:

"Turn then thy face in the direction of the Sacred Mosque. Wherever you are, turn your faces in that direction [for prayers]."

(2:144)

The direction from any place on the globe toward the Ka'aba is known as *qibla*.

The Ka'aba was the first structure built by man consecrated to the worship of One God. It was erected in antiquity by the Prophet Ibrahim and his son Ismael (peace be on them). Qur'an refers to the building of the Ka'aba in several verses:

"And when We assigned to Ibrahim the site of the House.." (22:26) — "And when Ibrahim and Ismael were raising the foundations of the House (they prayed): 'Our Sustainer! Accept Thou this from us. Surely Thou art All-Hearing, All-Knowing...' " — (2:127) "And We commanded Ibrahim and Ismael: 'Purify My House for those who visit it and those who meditate therein, and those who bow down and prostrate.' " (2:125) — "And call to mind the occasion when Ibrahim said: 'My Sustainer! Make this city secure and save me and my descendants from worshipping idols.' "

(14:35)

However, in the course of time, the belief in the Oneness of God, the concept of submission to him, the significance of the Ka'aba and the spiritual aspect of *hajj* faded out of people's minds. They reverted to idol worship and superstitious pagan customs. Before the coming of Prophet Muhammad (peace be on him), there were 360 idols in Ka'aba and pilgrimage to it had degenerated into a mere funfair. When the Meccans submitted to Islam in 8 A.H. (After *Hijra*), the Prophet cleared the Ka'aba of all the idols and revived the true spirit of *hajj* according to God's command.

The Ka'aba

131

It should be stressed that the Ka'aba is not the birthplace of Prophet Muhammad and that pilgrimage to Ka'aba does not in any way signify the worship of the Prophet (peace be on him) or any other human being, as pilgrimage does in some religions. We venerate the Ka'aba and the other holy places for their history and associations, but *not* for themselves. This cannot be emphasized too strongly, for God Most High alone is the object of our worship, in *hajj* as in any other form of Islamic worship.

5. HAJJ – AN OBLIGATION *(FARD)*

Hajj is the Fifth Pillar of Islam. It is obligatory *(fard)* at at least once in a lifetime for any Muslim man or woman who fulfills the following conditions: at the time he (or she) intends to perform *hajj*, he should be sane, in sound health, free from debts, and should have enough resources not only to defray his own travel expenses but also to take care of his dependents who have remained at home. It is a further condition that peace and security for his life and property exist on the way to Mecca and back. God says in the Qur'an:

"And pilgrimage to the House [Ka'aba] is a duty people owe to God, for him who can afford the journey." (3:97)

If a Muslim dies without ever having performed *hajj*, any of his dependents or any other person whom they select can perform *hajj* on behalf of the deceased, if he fulfills the above requirements at the time of his death. A sick or disabled person who otherwise meets these requirements may choose another person to perform *hajj* on his behalf. At each stage of *hajj* the substitute person first performs the observances of *hajj* for himself and then again on behalf of the person whom he represents.

6. 'UMRA (THE MINOR PILGRIMAGE), HAJJ (THE MAJOR PILGRIMAGE), AND HAJJU AT-TAMATTU' (THE INTERRUPTED PILGRIMAGE)

(1) *'UMRA*: Any Muslim may visit Mecca at any time and perform *'umra*, the Minor Pilgrimage. This consists of putting on *ihram* (the pilgrim's dress) and performing *tawaf* and *sa'ai* (see Section 7). The *ihram* is taken off after *sa'ai*. *'Umra* is

complete in itself, and it is not a substitute for *hajj*, the Major Pilgrimage.

(2) *HAJJ*: The observances of *hajj* are concentrated on 8th, 9th and 10th of Dhul-Hijja. These consist of putting on *ihram*, performing *tawaf* and *sa'ai*, taking part in the observances at Arafat, Muzdalifa and Mina, and the sacrifice of *Eid-ul-Adha*.

On the basis of *sunnah* (the practice of the Prophet, peace be on him), it is the general practice to include *'umra* in performing *hajj*. This is done simply by including *'umra* in the intention (*niyat*) (see Section 7 (1)).

(3) *HAJJU AT-TAMATTU'*: If one wishes, he may arrive in Mecca—as early as the beginning of the month of Shawwal, perform *'umra*, put aside *ihram*, and then wait to perform *hajj* at the speficied time in Dhul-Hijja. This is called *hajju at-tamattu'*, the Interrupted Pilgrimage.

The months of Shawwal, Dhul-Qu'da and the first twelve days of Dhul-Hijja (the tenth, eleventh and twelfth months of the Islamic calendar) are specified for *hajj*. This means that one could come to Mecca for *hajju at-tamattu'* at any time between the beginning of Shawwal and the days specified for *hajj*, while for *hajj* alone one would arrive in the early part of Dhul-Hijja. As the Islamic calendar is regulated by the lunar cycle, these months rotate through different seasons of the solar year.

7. THE OBSERVANCES OF HAJJ

The obligatory (*fard*) observances of *hajj*, together with their historical significance, will be described here briefly in the order in which they are performed.

(1) *IHRAM*, the physical and spiritual state of consecration to God: Before approaching Mecca, the pilgrim takes a full bath (*ghusl*) if possible (or he may perform ablution — *wudu* or *tayammum* — if it is not possible), before putting on the garments of *ihram*. In *ihram* attire, he expresses his intention (*niyat*) by saying:

133

> "O God, I intend to perform *hajj* (or *'umra, tamattu'*, or *'umra* with
> *hajj*, as the case may be), and I am taking *ihram* for it. Make it
> easy for me, and accept it it from me."

The putting-on of *ihram* is followed by a two-*rakat* (two-unit)
prayer *(salat)* .

The *ihram* dress, which all male pilgrims wear, consists
of two sheets of ordinary unsewn white cloth, one covering the
lower part of the body to the ankles and the other draped over
one shoulder, covering the upper half of the body. While
there is no specific *ihram* for women, they should put on clean,
plain clothing at the time of entering *ihram*, wearing long-
sleeved garments which reach to the ankles and covering their
hair.

Ihram signifies a state of peace, self-denial and total
submission to God. The putting on of the pilgrim's dress is
symbolic of renouncing worldly and material goals and vanities.
The pilgrim who is in a state of consecration (*muhrim*) must
abstain even from ordinarily lawful satisfactions and pleasures
until the observances of *hajj* are over and *ihram* is put aside.
In the state of *ihram*, he may not use any other form of dress,
jewelry or personal adornments, perfume or scent, may not
shave, trim his hair or nails, or engage in marital intercourse.
During the days in *ihram* there may be no wrangling or argu-
ment, no rudeness, no discussion of the opposite sex, no up-
rooting of any growing thing, and no hunting. Bodily, the
pilgrim is to be devoted to the acts of the pilgrimage; spiritually
he or she is to be concerned with the worship of Almighty
God, self-examination, an awareness of the meaning of his
devotional acts and words, and a sense of the brotherhood and
unity of all Muslims.

From the beginning of the observances until the first
pillar is stoned at Mina (see Section 5), the pilgrim makes many
devotional calls (*talbiya*). These calls are said aloud, in unison
with one's fellow pilgrims at each state of the observances.

(2) *TAWAF* (going around):   On entering the great
courtyard which encircles the Ka'aba, the pilgrim recites:
> "O God, Thou are Peace, and peace comes from Thee, so, our
> Sustainer, give us peace and admit us to the Garden, the Abode
> of Peace [Paradise]."

He then walks around the Ka'aba seven times, starting his circuits from the corner of the Black Stone (*al-Hajar al-Aswad*), a relic from the original structure of the Sacred Ka'aba built by Abraham, after kissing, touching or raising his hand toward the Black Stone, according to the practice (*sunnah*) of the Holy Prophet (peace be on him). During each of the seven circuits, different recitations are said, the pilgrims in groups repeating the prayers after the pilgrim guide who is the leader of their group. If one cannot follow the words of the guide, he may praise God in his own words.

(3) *SA'AI* (hastening): On completion of the circuits of the Ka'aba, the pilgrim proceeds toward as-Safa and al-Marwa, two small hills situated nearby in the center of Mecca. Long ago, the Prophet Ibrahim, at the command of God, left his wife Hajer and his son Ismael (peace be on them) here with a small supply of food and water, to live in the deserted land of Mecca. Their ration of food and water was soon gone. The scorching desert sun created an intense thirst in the unsheltered child and his mother. Hajer ran up and down as-Safa and al-Marwa to see if she could find water for her distressed child. Meanwhile, the boy had dug his heels into the sand, and when Hajer returned to him, water was welling up from the floor of the desert at his feet. With the precious liquid she quenched the thirst of her son, who was near death. Because of this well, which continued to flow, a group of tribesmen settled in the valley of Mecca near 'Hajer and Ismael. The spring, known as the Well of Zamzam, has been in existence ever since, although its location was later lost. It was eventually discovered again by Abdul Muttalib, the grandfather of Prophet Muhammad (peace be on him), when its location was shown to him by God in a dream. The Well of Zamzam is held in great reverence, and pilgrims drink from it during their pilgrimage.

God has prescribed the remembrance of Hajer's attempts to find water (*sa'ai*) as an important part of the observances of *hajj*. Each pilgrim ascends as-Safa. At the top he makes devotional calls (*talbiya*), descends from the hill, walks the distance to al-Marwa and climbs it, making similar *talbiya*, repeating *sa'ai* seven times.

135

(4) *ARAFAT* and *MUZDALIFA*: After sunrise on 9th of Dhul-Hijja, the pilgrim sets out for Mount Arafat (about thirteen miles distant), either on foot or by conveyance, reciting *talbiya*. The valley of Arafat is a great barren plain large enough to contain the entire assembly of pilgrims, who in recent years have numbered several hundred thousand. Here, at high noon on 9th of Dhul-Hijja, all the pilgrims rise to their feet to worship their Lord, examine themselves, declare their repentance, and realize the true meaning of the brotherhood of all Muslims. Here *Dhuhr* and *'Asr* prayers are performed in congregation. The Holy Prophet (peace be on him) has said concerning these prayers, "The best of prayers is the prayer of the day of Arafat." Just after sunset, all the pilgrims break camp and hurry to Muzdalifa, about five miles distant, where everyone performs *Maghrib* and *'Isha* prayers and passes the the night.

Arafat

(5) *MINA*: On the morning of 10th of Dhul-Hijja, the pilgrims return to Mina, a small village which was passed earlier on the way from Mecca to Arafat. In Mina there are three stone pillars representing three positions where the devil (Satan) tried to tempt Prophet Ismael (peace be on him) to rebellion when his father was leading him to the place of sacrifice (see

Section 2).   Ismael drove away the devil by throwing stones at him, and in Mina the pilgrims throw stones which they have gathered at the three pillars to signify the rejection of evil promptings.

(6) *EID-UL-ADHA* (The Feast of Sacrifice): After stoning the first of the three pillars, the pilgrims sacrifice a sheep, goat or camel, following the practice *(sunnah)* of the Prophet Ibrahim who sacrificed a ram when God spared him the sacrifice of his son Ismael (peace be on them). While *Eid-ul-Adha* is actually a part of the observances of *hajj*, it is also celebrated throughout the Muslim world, and every Muslim who can afford it sacrifices an animal on this occasion. Part of the meat is distributed among the poor and needy for food, and the remainder is used to feed the household and shared with relatives and friends.

It should be pointed out that the word 'sacrifice' used in this context does not have the usual meaning of atonement for sin or an attempt to appease an angry deity. It signifies the remembrance of the willingness of Ibrahim (peace be on him) to sacrifice his own desires and attachments in submission to God, and it serves as a reminder to Muslims that they should be ready, if required, to sacrifice everything they have — even their lives — in the cause of God and his religion. God says in the Qur'an:

> "It is not their meat nor blood that reaches God. It is your piety that reaches Him. He has made them [animals] subject to you that you might glorify God for His guidance to you. And proclaim the good tidings to all who do right." (22:37)

After this, the pilgrims shave, snip or cut off a few strands of hair, which signifies the end of wearing *ihram* dress, although all the prohibitions of *ihram* apart from returning to ordinary dress are in effect until after the second circuiting *(tawaf ifadha)* of the Ka'aba which is performed on 10th of Dhul Hijja or the following day. Its completion releases the pilgrims from the prohibitions of *ihram*. The pilgrims remain in the valley of Mina for two or three days after 10th of Dhul-Hijja worshipping God, and additional stonings of the pillars take place during this time. Some pilgrims spend most of the day in Mecca, returning to Mina only at night; but all must remain in Mina

137

for at least two nights following the night of the 10th. The observances of *hajj* are complete by 13th of Dhul-Hijja.

Most of the pilgrims visit Medina, where Prophet Muhammad's Tomb and Mosque *(al-Masjid al-Nabawi)* are located. Some also visit *al-Aqsa* (the Farthest Mosque) in Jerusalem, sacred to Muslims because of its connection with the Night of the Journey and because of its connection with the Night of the Journey and the Ascension (*Lailat al-Isra wa al-Mi'raj*) (see Unit 10: Muslim Holidays and Ceremonies, Section 2 (4)). These visits (*ziara*), however, are not obligatory and are not part of the observances of *hajj*.

The Prophet's Mosque

8. PRACTICAL SUGGESTIONS

The details of the observances of *hajj* and *'umra* are intricate and lengthy, and may be found in any standard book on the subject, such as "The Sacred Journey" by Ahmad Kamal, from which most of the material in this unit is taken. Any Muslim intending to go on *hajj* or *'umra* must obtain a valid visa from the Embassy of Saudi Arabia. One can obtain the service of a professional guide, licensed by the Saudi government, who is responsible for the material and spiritual welfare of the pilgrims under his care and who also acts as interpreter for pilgrims who do not speak Arabic.

In the name of Allah, the Beneficent, the Merciful

1. THE MEANING OF MORALITY

The dictionary defines morality as meaning "the right or wrong of an action; set of rules of conduct based on the principle of right conduct rather than on law or custom." First we note that the words 'right,' 'wrong,' 'good,' 'bad ' and 'evil' are terms denoting value judgments, while terms like 'charity,' 'humility,' 'truthfulness ' and 'justice' are descriptive terms, designating a particular attitude or mode of behavior. Whether a particular attitude or action - for example, modesty - is considered good or bad depends upon the criterion by which human actions are to be judged. In Islam, this criterion is Qur'an and *Sunnah* (the practice of Prophet Muhammad, peace be on him). However, in the final analysis actions are judged by God according to the intentions behind them. No matter how apparently beneficial an act may be, if the doer does not believe in God and is not striving to obey and to please Him by acting within the framework of His laws, the act has been done for some reason other than for the sake of God and its true worth remains questionable.

2. THE FOUNDATION OF ISLAMIC MORALITY: FAITH

The teaching of Islam outlines a way of life based on faith (*iman*) and good deeds (*salihat*). Qur'an says:

"Time is the witness! Indeed, man is at loss, except those who have faith and do good deeds, counselling each other of truth and counselling each other of patience." (103:1-3)

Faith is not merely a proclamation of belief in the reality

139

of God and the truth of His messenger Muhammad (peace be on him), but also the putting of our beliefs into practice by fulfilling our obligations both to God and to man. Clearly one's obligations to his Creator and Sustainer ought to take precedence over all other obligations. Qur'an emphasizes this point thus:

> "Say: If your fathers, sons, brothers, wives and relatives, the wealth which you have acquired, the commerce in which you fear decline, and the dwellings in which you delight are dearer to you than God and His messenger and striving in His cause, then wait until God brings about His decree; and God does not guide the rebellious." (9:24)

A believer's faith and trust in God are expressed in his intentions, attitudes, words and deeds. He proclaims his beliefs, remembers God often with an attitude of thankfulness, humility and love, purifies his intentions, and practices the commandments of God and the *Sunnah* of His prophet and teaches them to others. Qur'an exhorts:

> "Obey God and His messenger, if you are believers." (8:1,20)

Obedience to God is not confined to personal piety, but extends to all spheres of personal, social, economic and international affairs. Each individual Muslim, as well as the entire community of Muslims, has the obligation to strive for the establishment of the moral laws of God on earth.

According to Qur'an, the present life is only a testing ground for man, while the life Hereafter is the ultimate goal.

> "Wealth and children are the adornments of this world. But the enduring things - deeds of righteousness - are better with God in reward, and better in hope." (18:46)

Thus a believer always remains conscious that he will ultimately return to the Merciful and Just God to give an accounting of what he did in this life. The love of God, joy in His good pleasure, hope of His mercy, and fear of His justice, all combine in a believer to make his living of the present life the basis for the future life of unlimited duration.

> "O soul at peace! Return unto thy Sustainer, well-pleased, well-pleasing! Enter thou among My servants. Enter thou My Paradise." (89:28-30)

On the other hand, those who do not believe in the afterlife, or are too absorbed in the present to care about the future,

consider the successes and pleasures of this world their ultimate
goal.

"Verily, those who do not expect the meeting with Us and are
well-pleased with the life of the present world and feel at home
in it [as if there were no Hereafter], and those who are heedless
of Our signs, their abode will be the fire, because of what they
earned." (10:7-8)

One of the characteristics of a believer is his attitude of
humility and thankfulness. Man, as God's creature, owes everything - his very existence and subsistence — to God's boundless
mercy. It is both our obligation and our natural inclination to
be grateful for all the bounties which God continually showers
upon us. Our thankfulness to God is to be expressed not only
through words of praise and acts of worship, but also through
sharing God's gifts — wealth, knowledge, skills and attainments —
with others. In direct contrast to the attitude of a believer,
ingratitude for God's gifts, self-righteousness, and pride of any
kind — for example, in one's achievements, wealth, position,
family background, race or national origin — are expressions
of a lack of understanding of man's position in the world and
of God's infinite power and goodness, or even of unbelief.
Qur'an says:

"As for the believers who do good deeds, He will pay them
their wages, and He will give them more from His bounty. As for
those who are disdainful and proud, He will punish them with
a grevious penalty; nor will they find, besides God, any to protect
or help them." (4:173)

"If We give man a taste of mercy from Us, and then withdraw it
from him, behold! he becomes desperate and ungrateful. But if we
let him taste prosperity after hardship that has visited him, he is
sure to say: 'The evils have gone from me.' Behold, he is exultant,
boastful, except such as are patient and do good deeds. For them
is forgiveness and a great reward." (11:9-11)

The Objective of Islamic Teachings: A Balanced Life

Qur'an tells us that every man is born with pure faith —
hanif (the word also used to describe the faith of the Prophet
Abraham, peace be on him, in Qur'an 2:135), the original
pattern according to which God created mankind.

"So set thy direction to the pure faith, the pattern of God on which He has made mankind." (30:30)

That is to say, it is part of man's basic nature to believe in the Oneness of God and to be inclined toward good deeds. Qur'an also says:

"We indeed created man in the best of patterns." (95:4)

In this respect Islam's view of man contrasts with those religions which burden man's soul with 'original sin' or consider man's physical needs and biological desires to be obstacles to be his spiritual aspirations.

Islam takes an integrated and wholesome view of man, recognizing that his personality is indivisible. As a matter of emphasis or for the purpose of discussion, we may speak of the spiritual, intellectual, emotional, biological and other aspects of man's personality, but all these aspects are in fact inseparable from one another. Thus Islam does not recognize a division and a duality between religious and secular, between 'sacred and profane,' between spiritual and material, between what is done with the thought of God and what is done with God put out of one's mind. When Qur'an prescribes acts of worship — prayer, fasting, poor-due, pilgrimage — these acts contain and imply physical, emotion, intellectual, social and material benefits for Muslims. When it sets forth some injunction concerning practical matters - for example, business transactions, trade, administration of justice, the practice of usury, marriage and divorce, eating and drinking, and so on — it does not neglect the spiritual aspect of man.

A truly balanced and God-conscious life, then, is an equilibrium of the various aspects of human existence, not stifling one part and placing too much emphasis on the other. Praying, fasting, reading Qur'an and other devotional acts are very basic and essential aspects of a Muslim's life, but they must go hand-in-hand with other basic and essential aspects of his life, all being done with the same spirit of God-consciousness and striving to please Him. A Muslim is not asked nor expected to destroy his natural desires and inclinations, but to make every aspect of himself Muslim, disciplining his desires and inclinations to come within the limits set by God.

Since in Islam, as it has been pointed out, there are no specifically 'sacred' acts, no sacraments or rites requiring a special class of ordained individuals to perform them, Islam does not have, nor does it require, any priestly class to administer the spiritual affairs of Muslims. All human affairs are considered to be the joint responsibility of all the people, while each individual is responsible for seeing that he personally does not transgress the limits prescribed by God. Quran exhorts:

"Let there arise out of you a group of people inviting to all that is good, enjoining what is right and forbidding what is wrong: they are the successful." (3:104)

The practical significance of this injunction is that each Muslim should try his best to learn what God has enjoined and forbidden, to act upon it, to teach it to others, and to strive to establish God's laws on earth.

Qur'an asks people to use their reason and understanding in approaching God and in living their lives. To imitate the behavior of others in the society without thinking, just because "everybody does it," is not permissible for a Muslim. Qur'an says:

"Only the learned among people truly fear God." (35:28)

and the Holy Prophet (peace be on him) has said:

"The search for knowledge is an obligation on every Muslim, man and woman."

The meaning of these statements is that to live without using one's understanding, without reflection, even if one is sincere, is not enough. Sincerity of heart must be accompanied by understanding of mind.

The Infinite Wisdom of the Divine Laws

As Muslims, we realize that God's injunctions are not arbitary, whimsical, despotic or impossible to act upon. On the contrary, God in His infinite wisdom and mercy has outlined certain moral laws in order to meet the needs of man, physical as well as spiritual, and these laws are constant and immutable, just as are the 'natural laws' of God which govern the rest of His creation. Because the total nature of man is known only to his Creator, these laws are timeless and universal, taking into consideration all aspects of man's condition, avoiding extremes and outlining a middle path.

Disobedience to any of these moral principles necessarily results in some form of corruption within a society. We can see examples of this in the history of nations and civilizations which have passed away, and the present-day world is full of all kinds of examples. In whatever sphere people follow the moral principles given by God — whether they are aware of doing so or not — the beneficial results are apparent. If, even in the same society, some of other of these principles are not followed, the harmful effects are equally obvious. Indeed, it is possible, as we have seen again and again in our time, for one individual who has enough power to cause great harm to a society or even to destroy it by disregard for the Divine laws of morality. Throughout the world today we see the proliferation of such problems as class barriers and mutual hatreds, wars of national interest, racial strife, unbridled materialism, increases in crime, disruption of family life, sexual license, addiction to drugs and alcohol, and so on, with all their evil effects on individuals and society, all equally the result of disobedience to the moral laws given by God.

On the other hand, living according to the laws of God brings peace, harmony and stability to the individual, no matter what his external circumstances may be. For human society, then, adherence to these principles has the effect of transforming people from self-seeking, greedy, proud, unjust and dishonest individuals into a community of brothers and sisters living together in mutual respect, harmony, co-operation and consideration of one another's welfare. Co-operation rather than competition for existence, service to others rather than exploitation, mutual consultation rather than domination, are the guiding principles of Islam in social, economic and political affairs. In the way of life of Prophet Muhammad (peace be on him) and his Companions, we see a clear example of this ideal community, perhaps for the only and unique time in the history of the world. God willing, such a community can again come into being if Muslims join together in faithfully following what God has enjoined.

Let us turn now to Qur'an and *Sunnah* to see what some of the moral teachings of Islam are in regard to the various aspects of man's life — that is, his personal character, inter-

144

personal relationships, social responsibilities, economic and administrative affairs, and his striving in the cause of God.

Personal Character

Since the quality of a society depends upon the quality of the individuals who are its members, we will discuss personal character first.

Among the teachings of Islam, great emphasis is laid on God-consciousness, which is an approximate translation of the word *taqwa*. *Taqwa* refers to an attitude of mind, the awareness of God and consciousness of one's responsibility to Him. As such, it is mentioned in Qur'an as being the foundation of a Muslim's character.

> ★The most honorable among you in the sight of God is the one who is most God-conscious. (49:13)

God-consciousness provides man with a sound conscience.

> ★O you who believe! If you remain conscious of God, He will grant you a criterion (to judge between right and wrong). . . (8:29)
> ★★The Prophet (peace be on him) has said: If, through fear of God, tears — even a small drop — fall from any believer's eyes, he will be kept away from Hell by God.

This *hadith* clarifies how unmistakably the conduct of man is governed by his awareness of his responsibility to God, and how even a small element of this awareness in a man's heart can make the greatest difference in his life, both here and and Hereafter.

In the teachings of Islam, great emphasis is placed on humility, modesty, control of passions and desires, truthfulness, integrity, patience and steadfastness. We are enjoined to fulfill all our promises and contracts, to keep all trusts, to meet our engagements, and to repay our debts. We now give some passages from Qur'an which cover the broad spectrum of personal moral conduct.

> ★For in God's sight are His servants — . . . those who are patient, truthful, devout, who spend in charity, and who pray for forgiveness at daybreak. (3:15, 17)
> ★And God loves those who are firm and steadfast. (3:146)
> ★And vie with one another to attain to your Sustainer's forgiveness and to a Paradise as vast as the heavens and the earth, which awaits the God-conscious, who spend for charity in time of plenty and in time of hardship, and restrain their anger, and par-

don their fellow men, for God loves those who do good; who, when they have committed a shameful deed or have (otherwise) sinned against themselves, remember God and ask for forgiveness for their sins — for who but God could forgive sins? — and do not persist knowingly in doing whatever (wrong) they did. These it is who shall have as their reward forgiveness from their Sustainer, and gardens through which running waters flow, therein to abide: how excellent a reward for those who labor! (3:133-136)

*Make due allowance for man's nature, and enjoin the doing of what is right; and leave alone all those who choose to remain ignorant. And if it should happen that a prompting from Satan stirs thee up (to blind anger), seek refuge in God: behold, He is All-Hearing, All-Knowing. Verily, they who are conscious of God think (of Him) whenever any dark suggestion from Satan touches them — whereupon, lo! they begin to see clearly, even though their (godless) brethren would (like to) draw them into error: and then they cannot fail to do what is right. (7:199-201)

*And be satisfied with those who call upon their Sustainer morning and evening, seeking His countenance [that is, nearness to God]; and do not let your eyes pass beyond them, seeking the pomp and glitter of this life; and do not obey any whose heart We have permitted to neglect the remembrance of Us, one who follows his own desires, whose case has gone beyond all bounds. (18:28)

*You shall certainly be tried and tested in your possessions and in your personal selves; and you shall certainly hear much that will grieve you, from those who received the Scripture before you and from the polytheists. But if you persevere patiently and remain conscious of God, then that will be the determining factor in all affairs. (3:186)

*Establish regular prayer, enjoin what is just, and forbid what is wrong; and bear patiently whatever may befall you; for this is true constancy. And do not swell your cheek (with pride) at men, nor walk in insolence through the earth, for God does not love any man proud and boastful. And be moderate in your pace and lower your voice; for the harshest of sounds, indeed, is the braying of the ass. (31:18-19)

*For Muslim men and women, for believing men and women, for devout men and women, for true men and women, for patient men and women, for humble men and women, for charitable men and women, for men and women who fast, for men and women who guard their chastity, for men and women who engage much in

God's praise — for them God has prepared forgiveness and great reward. (33:35)

★And do not cover truth with falsehood, nor conceal the truth when you know (what it is). (2:42)

★— Those who keep their plighted faith and remain conscious of God — verily, God loves those who remain conscious of Him. (3:76)

★O you who believe! Fulfill all obligations. (5:1)

God has forbidden certain things which are indecent or harmful. It is our responsibility to abstain from them, and we should in fact try to avoid situations which lead to temptation. God says:

★Do not come near to illicit sexual relations; surely it is an indecency and an evil way. (17:32)

★Let those who do not find the means for marriage keep themselves chaste, until God gives them the means out of His grace. (24:33)

★★The Prophet (peace be on him) has said: Modesty and faith are both companions; when one is taken away the other is taken.

★O you who believe! intoxicants and games of chance [gambling] and idolatrous practices and the divining of the future are but a loathsome evil of Satan's doing: shun it, then, so that you might be graced with good everlasting. By means of intoxicants an games of chance Satan seeks only to sow enmity and hatred among you and to turn you away from the remembrance of God and from the remembrance of God and from prayer. Will you not then desist? (5:93-94)

In Qur'an 5:4 the foods which are forbidden to Muslims are mentioned.

In a way which summarizes the moral behavior of a Muslim, the Prophet (peace be on him) said:

★★My Sustainer has given me nine commands: to remain conscious of God, whether in private or in public; to speak justly, whether angry or pleased; to show moderation both when poor and when rich; to reunite friendship with those who have broken it off with me; to give to him who refuses me; to forgive him who has wronged me; that my silence should be occupied with thought; that my looking should be an admonition; and that I should command what is right.

Interpersonal Relationships

If one were to summarize by one word the Islamic teaching regarding interpersonal relationships, it would be with the single Arabic work *hilm,* which in English means 'forbearance, kindness and forgiveness.' In day-to-day affairs, one comes in contact with all sorts of other human beings. Since all people have their limitations, their weaknesses, their mistakes and errors of judgment, it is arrogant and presumptuous on anyone's part to pass judgment on others, to be intolerant, to treat people with contempt, or to mock or humiliate anyone.

> *. . .[Those who] restrain their anger, and pardon their fellow men, for God loves those who do good. . . (3:134)
>
> *Nor can good be equal to evil; repel (evil) with what is better; then he, between whom and your was enmity, will become as close friend. (41:34)
>
> *Kind words and the covering of faults are better than charity followed by injury. (2:263)
>
> **The Prophet (peace be on him), on being asked how many times one ought to forgive his servant's mistakes, said: Seventy times a day. Then he added: If you cannot bear your servant's weakness, release him from your service.

It is part of forbearance and kindness to refrain from gossip, from prying into the affairs of others, and from saying anything behind a person's back which he would not like to have said about himself. We are not to discuss the affairs of other people secretly except when it is with a view of doing them some good. The faults of others, if known to us, should be concealed rather than exposed. We are not to shame others, as it generates a response of defiance and guilt rather than the real awareness of error. We are to refrain from passing judgment on the quality of others' faith and sincerity. We are enjoined not to talk about evil deeds or happenings except in cases where some social action is required; and we should remove ourselves from any conversation in which things are discussed which are filthy, degrading or make a joke of religion.

> *O you who believe! Let not some men among you mock at other men: it may be that the (latter) are better than the (former); nor let some women mock at other women; it may be that the (latter) are better than the (former); and do not defame nor be sarcastic to each other, nor call each other by (offensive) nicknames: ill-seeming is a name connoting wickedness (to be used of one) after he has believed; and those who do not desist are (indeed) doing wrong. O you who believe! Avoid suspicion as much (as possible): for sus-

picion in some cases is a sin; and do not spy on each other, nor speak ill of each other behind their backs. . . Verily, the most honored of you in the sight of God is the one who is most God-conscious. And God has full knowledge and is well-acquainted (with all things). (49:11-13)

*In most of their secret talks there is no good: but if one exhorts to a deed of charity or justice or conciliation between men, (secrecy is permissible): to him who does this, seeking the good pleasure of God, We shall soon give a reward of highest value. (4:114)

*God does not love that evil should be openly mentioned, unless it be by him who has been wrong (thereby). (4:148)

*O you who believe! If a wicked person comes to you with any news, ascertain the truth, lest you harm people unwittingly, and afterwards become full of repentance for what you have done. (49:6)

**The Prophet (peace be on him) has said: The proof of a Muslim's sincerity is that he pays no heed to that which is not his business.

**The Prophet has also said: The Muslim is he from whose tongue and hand the Muslims are safe.

Social Responsibilities

The teachings of Islam concerning social responsibilities are based on kindness and consideration of others. Since a broad injunction to be kind is likely to be ignored in specific situations, Islam lays emphasis on specific acts of kindness and defines the responsibilities and rights of various relationships. In a widening circle of relationships, then, our first obligation is to our immediate family — parent, husband or wife and children, then to other relatives, neighbors, friends, and acquaintances, orphans and widows, the needy of the community, our fellow Muslims, all our fellow human beings, and animals.

1. **Parents:** Respect and care for parents is very much stressed in th Islamic teaching and is a very important part of a Muslims expression of faith.

*Your Sustainer has decreed that you worship none but Him, and that you be kind to parents. Whether one or both of them attain old age in your lifetime, do not say to them a word of contempt nor repel them, but address them in terms of honor. And, out of kindness, lower to them the wing of humility and say: "My Sustainer! Bestow on them Thy mercy, even as they cherished me in

childhood." (17:23-24, also 31:14)
**A man came to the Prophet (peace be on him) and asked:
Messenger of God, who is most deserving of good care from me?
The Prophet replied: Your mother (repeating it three times), then
your father, then your nearest relatives in order.

2. Husband, wife and children: God has made men responsible for their wives and children in the matters of providing them with the necessities, creating and maintaining a religious atmosphere in the home, and for their education and welfare. Women are responsible for the domestic well-being of their husbands and children and for the training of children. Mutual love and trust, keeping private what is personal between them, forgiving one another's weaknesses, and affection, warmth and kindness to each other are enjoined on both husband and wife. Children are to be helpful, respectful and obedient to their parents.

*Men shall take full care of women with the bounties which God
has bestowed more abundantly on some of them than on others,
and with what they may spend out of their possessions. And the
righteous women are the devout ones, who guard the intimacy
which God has (ordained to be) guarded. (4:34)
*They [wives] are your garments and you are their garments.
(2:187)
**The Prophet (peace be on him) has said: Among the believers
who show most perfect faith are those who have the best
position and are kindest to their families.

3. Other relatives: These come next in the line of those for whom a Muslim has responsibility. God says concerning blood ties:

*And render to the relatives their due rights, as (also) to those in
want, and to the traveller; and do not squander your wealth in the
manner of a spendthrift. (17:26)
*They ask thee what they should spend (in charity). Say: Whatever of your wealth you spend shall be for the parents and for
the near of kin and the orphans and the needy and the traveller;
and whatever good you do, verily, God has full knowledge thereof.
(2:215)

4. Neighbors: A person's character is seen in its true light by his neighbors. It is the duty of a Muslim to show particular kindness to his neighbors and to offer them as much help as he can.

★★A man asked the Prophet (peace be on him): Messenger of God, how can I know when I do well and when I do ill? The Prophet replied: When your neighbors say you have done well, you have done well; and when you hear them say you have done ill, you have done ill.

★★The Prophet also said: He is not a believer who eats his fill when his neighbor beside him is hungry; and: He does not believe from whose injurious conduct his neighbor is not safe.

5. **Orphans and widows:** Orphans and widows, in every society, need special care and provision. Although a widow may be averse to remarriage with the thought of remaining faithful to her husband's memory, still it is recommended that she should marry again.

★★The Prophet (peace be on him) has said: He who strives on behalf of a widow and a poor person is like one who strives in God's path.

Similarly, it is the responsibility of the nearest relatives to take care of orphans as they would care for their own children. If there are no relatives or if for any reason they do not assume responsibility for the bereaved child, it is the obligation of some other Muslim individual or organization to take care of the child as tenderly as possible.

★And they ask thee about orphans. Say: To improve their condition is best. And if your share their life, they are your brothers, for God distinguishes between him who spoils things and him who improves. (2:220, also 4:2, 6, 10. 127, and 17:34)

★★The Prophet (peace be on him) has said: I and the one who takes responsibility for an orphan, whether of his own kin or of others, will be in Paradise thus: and he pointed his forefinger and the middle finger with a slight space between them.

6. **Those in Need:** *Zakat* (poor-due) is the Fourth Pillar of Islam, and it is obligatory upon every Muslim whose economic position qualifies him to pay it (see Unit 5—B, Poor-due). Apart from *Zakat*, charity is enjoined over and over again in Qur'an and *Hadith*. This means that to do what we can to help others who are in need is a very important and basic part of Islam. When Muslims of earlier times obeyed these injunctions faith-

151

fully, the general level of prosperity was at times so high that no one could be found who was in need of help from *Zakat* funds.

Acts of charity, whether involving material help or any other sort of giving, should be done in a generous and kind spirit and not followed by words which humiliate or create a sense of obligation.

★Those who spend their wealth in the way of God and do not thereafter mar their gifts with reminders of their generosity and hurting [the feelings of the recipients] shall have their reward with their Sustainer, and no fear need they have, neither shall they grieve. Kind words and forgiveness are better than charity followed by injury; and God is Self-Sufficient, Forbearing. (2:262-263)

★O you who believe! Spend on others out of the good things which you may have acquired, and out of that which We bring forth for you from the earth; and do not choose for your spending the bad things which you (yourselves) would not accept without averting your eyes in disbain. And know that God is Self-Sufficient, Most Praiseworthy. (2:267)

★They ask thee how much they are to spend [in the way of God]. Say: Whatever is beyond your needs. (2:219)

★And if you do deeds of charity openly, it is well; but if you bestow it upon the needy in secret, it will be even better for you, and it will atone for some of your bad deeds. And God is aware of all that you do . . . And whatever good you may spend on others is for your own good, provided that you spend only out of a longing for God's countenance [that is, nearness to God]: for whatever you may spend will be repaid unto you in full, and you shall not be wronged. (2:271, 273)

★By no means shall you attain righteousness unless you give (freely) of that which you love; and whatever you give, verily, God has full knowledge of it. (3:92)

★If the debtor is in difficulty, grant him time until it is easy for him to repay. But if you remit it by way of charity, that is best for you if you only knew. (2:280)

★★The Prophet (peace be on him) has said: If one gives justice between two men, it is charity; if one helps a man with his beast, loading or lifting his goods on it, it is charity; a good word is charity; every step one takes toward prayer is charity; if anyone removes anything injurious from the road it is charity.

★★The Prophet said that every Muslim must give charity. He was asked how this could apply to one who had nothing. The Prophet

152

replied that he should work with his hands, gaining benefit for himself thereby, and give charity. He was asked what would happen if he were unable to do this or did not do it. The Prophet replied that he should help one who was in need and sad. He was asked what he should do if he did not do that, and replied that he should enjoin what is good. He was asked what he should do if he did not do that, and he replied that he should refrain from evil, and that would be charity for him.

From these Qur'anic verses and *Hadiths* we see that the definition of charity is very broad and includes anything one does to benefit or to help others.

7. **Fellow Muslims:** Relationships among Muslims are of very great importance, for all Muslims throughout the world form one community of people submitting to God's laws and striving to please Him, mutually helping one another toward the goals of Islam. All Muslims are brothers and sisters to one another, and their behavior to each other should be that of members of a family, full of kindness and consideration.

*Verily, the believers are one brotherhood. (49:10)

*And hold fast to God's bond, all together, and do not draw apart from one another. (3:103)

**The Prophet (peace be on him) has said: The believers are like a single man; if his eye is affected, all of him is affected, and if his head is affected, all of him is affected.

**The Prophet has also said: One Muslim should do six acts of kindness to another: he should salute him when he meets him, accept his invitation when he gives one, say "God have mercy on you" (*"Yar hamak Allah"*) when he sneezes, visit him when he is sick, follow his bier when he dies, and like for him what he likes for himself.

**The Prophet has also said: A Muslim is a Muslim's brother; he does not wrong him or abandon him. If anyone cares for his brother's need, God will care for his need; if anyone removes his brother's anxiety, God will remove from him one of the anxieties on the Day of Judgment; and if anyone conceals a Muslim's secrets God will conceal his secrets on the Day of Judgment.

8. **Fellow Men:** In God's sight a person is judged only by his intentions and his actions. Considerations of birth, national origin, racial background, material success, social status, and so on, all have no consequence in the sight of God. As

Muslims, therefore, we should treat all persons with fairness and kindness without regard to any of these man-made distinctions and differences.

> *O mankind! We have created you from a male and a female, and made you into races and tribes that you may know one another. Verily, the most honorable among you in the sight of God is the one who is most God-conscious. And God is All-Knowing, All-Aware. (49:13)

> **The Prophet (peace be on him) has said: All creatures are God's children, and those dearest to God are the ones who treat His children kindly.

9. **Animals:** Kindness and good treatment should be extended to animals as well as to human beings. The Prophet (peace be on him) forbade Muslims to starve, torment or mutilate animals. This, however, is not a prohibition against killing animals for food, in as merciful a manner as possible, or against killing animals or insects which are harmful to man, such as snakes, scorpions, flies, mosquitoes, and so on.

> *There is not an animal on the earth, nor a bird that flies on its wings, but are communities like you. (6:38)

> **Once the Prophet (peace be on him) was on a journey with some of his Companions. He left them for a while, and some of the Companions saw a bird with two young ones and they took the young ones. The bird came and began to spread out its wings. When the Prophet returned, he said: Who has pained this one by the loss of her young? Give her young ones back to her.

Economic Affairs

According to Islam, God is Owner of all things, including those which human beings use and enjoy: land, crops, forests, oceans, minerals, and all other natural resources of this earth. Man, as vice-gerent of God on earth, is only a trustee. Thus a Muslim looks upon his wealth and material possessions as gifts and bounties from God, to be spent in ways pleasing to Him — that is, for satisfying the needs of oneself and one's immediate family, one's parents and relatives, orphans, widows, the poor and needy of the community, and for striving in the path of God. A livelihood is to be earned through any honest labor or productive investment. The acquired means is not to be hoarded nor wasted for purposes of show, nor used for

154

bribery or in any other way which results in injustice, oppression or harm to others. In the same spirit, the economic resources of a country are God's bounties to the people as a whole. These ought to be developed and utilized for the benefit of all the people and not merely for a few, and not to be diverted to uses which are harmful in any way. Sharing rather than exploiting, co-operation rather than competition, is the true spirit of Islam. That is why usury (interest on loans), gambling, hoarding, greed, covetousness, and using money in any way which is wasteful are among the things forbidden by God.

> *And do not consume your wealth among yourselves wrongly, neither proffer it to the judges [as a bribe] so that you may sinfully consume a portion of (other) people's wealth, and that knowingly. (2:188)

> *O you who believe! Do not devour usury, doubled and multiplied; but fear God, that you may prosper. (3:130)

> *For God does not love those who are proud and boastful, those who are miserly or enjoin miserliness on others, or hide the bounties which God has bestowed on them. . .(4:36)

> *O you who believe! Do not consume your wealth among yourselves wrongly, but let there be trade by mutual agreement. (4:29)

> *Do not make your hand tied to your neck (in miserliness), nor stretch it forth to its utmost reach so that you become blameworthy and destitute. (17:29)

> *Do not exult, for God does not love those who exult. But seek, stated term, set it down in writing . . . And call upon two of your with the (wealth) which God has bestowed on thee, the home of the Hereafter, and do not forget thy portion in this world: but do good, as God has been good to thee, and do not seek (occasions for) mischief in the land, for God does not love those who do mischief. (28:76-77)

In business transactions, honesty, trustworthiness and fair dealing are duties to God. Cheating, concealing the defects of merchandise, or taking advantage of someone's ignorance are prohibited to Muslims.

Many years before the prophethood was bestowed on Muhammad (peace be on him), he was given the title 'al-Amin' — 'The Trustworthy' — by the people of Mecca. His fair dealings in trade made such a deep impression on the widowed Khadijah, who had employed him, that she initiated the proposal of marriage to him, in spite of the fact that she was rich and he poor, and that she was many years older than he.

Concerning honesty and fair dealings, God says:

★And if one of you deposits something on trust with another, let the trustee discharge his trust, and fear his Sustainer. (2:283)

★Give full measure when you measure, and weigh with a straight balance. That is the most fitting and most advantageous in the final determination. (17:35)

★O you who believe! Whenever you give or take credit for a stated term, set it down in writing. . .And call upon two of your men to act as witnesses; and if two men are not available, then a man and two women from among such as are acceptable to you as witnesses, so that if one of them should make a mistake, the other could remind her . . .And do not disdain to write it [your contract] down, whether it be small or great, with its terms; that is more equitable in the sight of God, more reliable as evidence, and more likely to prevent you from having doubts (later). (2:282)

Administrative Affairs

Administrators and judges bear a great responsibility. Unless such persons have a consciousness of their obligations to God, it is possible that they may be swayed by pressure groups, self-interest or by their own prejudices and preferences to deviate from justice. God wishes to impress upon all human beings, whether they are responsible for a few persons or for a whole nation, that justice and fair dealing are duties to Him, and even national interest should not be allowed to interfere with this obligation.

★O you who believe! Be securers of justice, witnesses for God, and do not let the hatred of a people make you swerve to do wrong and depart from justice. Be just: that is nearer to God-consciousness; and fear God, for God is well-acquainted with all that you do. (5:9)

★O you who believe! Stand out firmly for justice, as witnesses for God, even as against yourselves, or your parents, or your kin, and whether it concerns rich or poor, for God can best protect both. Then do not follow caprice, lest you swerve, and if you twist or turn (from justice), verily God is well-acquainted with all that you do. (4:135)

While concern for the welfare of the people, justice and obedience to God's laws are the duty of a ruler or governing body, the ruled are in turn obliged to obey their ruler or government as long as it does not command them to do anything in disobedience to God's laws. The ruler or governing body is under obligation to consult with the people (or their representatives) in order to ascertain their views and needs.

★And consult among yourselves to settle affairs. (42:38)

★O you who believe! Obey God and the Messenger, and those who are charged with authority among you. (4:59)

★The Prophet (peace be on him) has said: Hearing and obeying are the duty of a Muslim both regarding what he likes and what he dislikes, as long as he is not commanded to perform an act of disobedience to God, in which case he must neither hear nor obey.

Jihad: Striving in the Cause of God

Jihad is an abbreviated way of saying '*jihad fi sabeel Allah*,' which means 'striving in God's cause.' This includes such efforts as teaching, explaining and expounding the message of Islam to others, working against evil and corruption, and joining forces with individuals or groups in combating injustice, social inequity, illiteracy, poverty, disease and other human problems. God says:

★Let there arise out of you a group of people inviting to all that is good, enjoining what is right, and forbidding what is wrong; they are the successful. (3:104)

★You are the best community raised (for the good) of mankind; you enjoin the doing of what is right and forbid the doing of what is wrong, and you believe in God. (3:110)

★O you who believe! Remain conscious of God, and seek to come near unto Him, and strive hard in His cause, so that you might be graced with good everlasting. (5:35)

★Do men think that they will be left alone on saying, "We believe," and that they will not be tested? (29:2)

★If anyone strives [in the cause of God], he does so for his own soul: for God does not need anything from His creation. (29:6)

Another aspect of striving in the path of God is emigration from a place where one is oppressed to such an extent that he cannot live and act as a Muslim to a place when this is possible.

★To those who leave their homes in God's cause, after suffering oppression, We will assuredly give a goodly home in this world; but truly the reward of the Hereafter will be greater, if they only realized (this). (16:41)

There are occasions, however, when it becomes necessary to take up arms against oppressors or aggressors. While forbid ing Muslims to commit aggression, God commands them to defend themselves against those who attack or oppress them.

*And fight in God's cause against those who wage war upon you; but do not commit aggression; verily God does not love aggressors. (2:190)

*To those against whom war is made, permission is given (to fight) because they are wronged; and, verily, God is most power- ful for their aid; (they are) those who have been expelled from their homes in defiance of right, only because they say, "Our Sustainer is God." If God did not check one set of people by means of another, there would surely have been pulled down monasteries, churches, synagogues and mosques, in which the name of God is commemorated in abundant measure. (22:40-41)

Conclusion

The moral teachings of Islam may be viewed in terms of an individual's rights and obligations in relation to other individuals. Although, as a matter of style, we have emphasized obligations, it is clear that what is seen as one person's obligation to another can also be seen as the latter's right on the former. Thus, 'parents have an obligation to their children' may also be stated as 'children have a right on their parents.'

It ought to be emphasized, however, that according to Islam the rights and obligations of an individual derive their authority from God and His Prophet (peace be on him), and not from any man-made system of ethics. The conduct prescribed by the Islamic teachings has much in common with other systems of ethics, but the spirit is different. For example, it is not peculiar to Islam that it asks for fairness and honesty in business transactions. What is unique in Islam is that, by insist- ing but fairness and honesty are obligations to God, it trans- forms an economic principle into a moral one. A Muslim business man, by being fair and honest, is not only benefitting from a sound business practice, but also deriving the spiritual benefit of following the commandment of God; while, if he cheats, he is not only violating his duty toward his fellow human beings but disoveying God as well.

In summary, then, the moral teachings of Islam define a person's obligations and rights in relation to others, emphasizing

158

that every obligation to others is, at the same time, an obligation to God. These teachings outline basic principles of conduct, such as honesty, justice, kindness and charity, which are as applicable in twentieth century America as they were in seventh century Arabia.

★And thou shalt not find any change in the law of God. (35:43)

In the name of Allah, the Beneficent, the Merciful

THE ISLAMIC CALENDAR

The Islamic calendar is reckoned from the year of *Hijrat*, i.e., the emigration of the Holy Prophet Muhammad (peace be on him) from Mecca to Medina, which occurred on 8th of Rabi' al-Awwal in the year 1 A.H. (After *Hijrat*). This reckoning was adopted during Umar's Caliphate at the suggestion of Ali, in 16 A.H., before which there was no fixed calendar in Arabia. I Muharram, the first day of the Islamic calendar year, is now generally celebrated by Muslims as *Hijrat* Day, although the actual *Hijrat* Day is 8 of Rabi' al-Awwal.

The Islamic calendar is based on the orbiting of the moon around the earth. A month is counted from the new moon to new moon. Since the average interval between consecutive similar phases of the moon is 29 days 12 hours 44 minutes, with a variation of one-half day, a lunar month consists of either 29 or 30 days. Thus the same month — for instance Ramadan — will have 29 days in some years and 30 days in others. There being twelve months in the year, the total number of days in a lunar year is always 353, 354 or 355. Any particular date of the lunar calendar travels *backward* through the solar calendar, completing a full cycle in about 33 years. January 31, 1968 A.C. (After Christ) corresponds to Dhul-Qu'da 1, 1387 A.H.

The name of the months of the Islamic calendar are:

1.	Muharram	2.	Safar
3.	Rabi' al-Awwal	4.	Rabi' al-Akhir
5.	Jamadi al-Awwal	6.	Jamadi al-Akhir
7.	Rajab	8.	Sha'ban
9.	Ramadan	10.	Shawwal
11.	Dhul-Qu'da	12.	Dhul-Hijja.

It may be mentioned that the date changes in the evening rather than at midnight. Thus the night of 27th of Rajab refers to the night *preceding* the twenty-seventh day.

1.   The Friday of each week is a special day. It significance is due to the obligatory (*fard*) congregational prayer, which will be described later.

2.   There are two celebrations which are *sunnah* (prescribed by the Prophet). These are:
   (a)   *Eid-al-Fitr* (The Festival of Fast-Breaking): 1st of Shawwal;
   (b)   *Eid-al-Adha* (The Festival of Sacrifice): 10th of Dhul-Hijja.

3.   Other occasions which are celebrated by Muslims are related to historical events. Their observance is neither *fard* (from Qur'an) nor *sunnah* (from the Prophet). These are:
   (a)   The Day of *Hijrat:* celebrated on 1st of Muharram, the first day of the year;
   (b)   *Meelad al-Nabi* (Birthday of the Holy Prophet): 12th of Rabi' al-Awwal;
   (c)   *Lailat al-Qadr* (The Night of Power): one of the odd-numbered nights of the last ten days of Ramadan;
   (d)   *Lailat al-Isra wa al-Mi'raj* (The Night of the Journey and the Ascension): the night of 27th of Rajab.

1.   Friday (Jum'a)

Friday — *Yawm al-Jum'a* (The Day of Assembly) in Arabic — is the day of obligatory congregational prayer (*salat*), and hence has a special religious and social significance for Muslims. While it is preferable to observe all the daily obligatory prayers (*salat*) in congregation, it is not required to do so. On the other hand, it is obligatory (*fard*) on every adult Muslim male to observe the Friday prayer in congregation. For women it is optional.

To prepare oneself for *Jum'a* prayer, one should take a shower or bath in the morning, put on clean clothes, and abstain from eating foods which leave an offensive odor on the breath, such as onions or garlic.

In Muslim countries, Friday prayer is always observed in mosques. However, in this country, where there are very few mosques, any place where people can gather is suitable for this purpose. It is the duty of Muslims residing in a community to

161

make some permanent arrangement for the observance of *Jum'a* prayer.

The *Jum'a* prayer, like any other congregational prayer, is led by an *imam* (leader), who is elected from among the gathering. The prayer is preceded by a sermon *(khutba)*, delivered by the *imam* who is leading the prayer. The sermon is a part of the worship and during it no one should pray, talk or do anything besides giving his full attention to the speaker. The sermon consists of two parts divided by a short interval. Current affairs, problems of Muslims (local or universal), a commentary on or explanation of Qur'anic passages or religious practices are suitable subjects for a sermon. Friday sermons have been and should continue to be a means of educating Muslims concerning their responsibilities and obligations, of keeping them abreast with current affairs, and of strengthening the spiritual bond between the believers. A sermon should begin and end with praise to God, blessings on the Prophet (peace be on him) and his Companions, and a supplication for all Muslims.

As Friday is the day of collective worship for Muslims, its observance may seem to resemble the Sabbath or Sunday in Judaism or Christianity. The similarity, however, is apparent rather than real. The basis of the Sabbath observances in these religions originated from the idea that as God the Creator "rested" on the seventh day after six days of "labor" at completing the creation of the heavens and the earth, so man should also rest in honor and observance of the Creator's "rest" (see Exodus 20:8-11). This idea is fundamentally contrary to the teachings or Islam, as the omnipotent God does not become weary and requires rest from His "work." There is no Sabbath in this sense in Islam. Muslims can carry on their usual activities and business before and after the Friday prayer. God says in Qur'an:

"O you who believe! When the call is proclaimed for prayer on Friday, hasten earnestly to the remembrance of God, and leave off business; that is best for you if you but knew. And when the prayer is finished, then you may disperse through the land and seek the bounty of God; and celebrate the praises of God often, that you may prosper." (62:9-10)

2. Festivals According to Sunnah

(a)   Eid-al-Fitr **(The Festival of Fast-Breaking)**
and
(b)   Eid-al-Adha   **(The Festival of Sacrifice)**

Eid means 'a recurring happiness or festivity.' There are two *Eids: Eid-al-Fitr,* celebrated on 1 Shawwal following the month of fasting, Ramadan, and *Eid-al-Adha,* celebrated on 10th of Dhul-Hijja, following the course of *hajj* (pilgrimage to Mecca).

When the Prophet (peace be on him) arrived in Medina, he found that the people of that city celebrated many festivals. He abolished these pagan observances and told the Muslims that God has prescribed only two festivals for them — the two *Eids.* The *Eids* are days of thanksgiving and rejoicing for every Muslim, as well as for the community of Muslims as a whole. *Eid-al-Fitr* celebrates the completion of a month of fasting and *Eid-al-Adha* the completion of *hajj,* both fasting and pilgrimage being acts of worship undertaken for the sake of God alone. (For details, see Unit 4: Fasting, and Unit 5a: Pilgrimage).

While the *Eids* are occasions for joy and happiness, they are certainly not occasions for frivolity, over-eating or the pursuit of pleasure. The joy which we feel on *Eid* is the spiritual joy of fulfilment — fulfilment of God's command of discipline, piety and collective worship. Each of the *Eid* days begins with prayer *(salat)* and is spent in alms-giving, visiting friends and relatives, and exchanging greetings and gifts. The spirit of *Eid* is the spirit of peace and forgiveness, for at these times one should forget all grudges and ill-feeling toward one's fellow men if he has not already done so. On *Eid* one makes fresh start in his relations with others in a brotherly spirit.

The time of *Eid* prayer is between sunrise and noon, and, like Friday prayer, *Eid* prayer is always said in congregation. If it is preferred, women may however, pray at home. One should bathe and put on clean clothes before coming to prayer. The *Eid* prayer consists of two *rakats* with six to sixteen additional *takbirs* (recitations of *"Allahu Akbar"* — God is Most Great), followed by a sermon *(khutba)* in two parts, similar to the Friday sermon. In the sermon of *Eid-al-Fitr,* the *imam* should draw the attention of the congregation to the

163

obligation of *sadaqat-al-fitr* (the charity of *Eid-al-Fitr;* see Unit 4: Fasting). In the sermon of *Eid-al-Adha,* he should emphasize the duty of sacrifice. The sacrifice of a lamb or sheep (for one household) or a cow (for seven households) is to be made on *Eid* day or during the following two days, i.e., on the 10th, 11th or 12th of Dhul-Hijja. A third of the meat is kept for the use of the household and the remainder is distributed un-cooked among the poor and sent as a gift to friends and relatives.

3. Celebrating of Historical Occasions

(a) *The Day of Hijrat* (The Emigration of Prophet Muhammad From Mecca to Medina)

Hijrat was the most significant event in the history of Islam. It marked the beginning of the success and spread of Islam. In Mecca the Muslims had been relentlessly persecuted, their lives and properties had not been safe, they had not been able to form a community or practice their religion openly, and they had not had any social or political influence. All these trials and difficulties were left behind when the Muslims, by God's permission, migrated to Medina. The people of Medina accepted Islam, taking the Prophet (peace be on him) as their guide and leader. Once they were secure from continued persecution (although not from repeated military attack), they organized themselves into a religious community, received the injunctions of God and acted upon them, practiced and preached their religion, and consolidated their strength. To commenorate *Hijrat,* the second Caliph, Umar, after consulting with the Companions of the Prophet, declared 1 Muharram of the year of *Hijrat* (July 15, 622 A.C.) to be the first day of the first year of the Islamic calendar.

Hijrat Day is celebrated by exchanging greetings and relating stories about the Prophet (peace be on him) and his Companions.

(b) *Meelad an-Nabi* (Birthday of the Prophet)

Meelad an-Nabi is the celebration of the birthday of the Holy Prophet (peace be on him). Muhammad was born on 12th of Rabi' al-Awwal 54 years before *Hijrat,* or August 20, 570 A.C., — a Monday — early in the morning.

From the point of view of Muslims, this date marks the most important event in the history of the world. Muhammad (peace be on him) was the "Seal of the Prophets" (Qur'an 33:40) and the bearer of Qur'an, God's final and complete message to mankind. His conduct is an example for everyone of all times and places to follow. Through him God perfected His religion, Islam, and enlightened man concerning His purpose for humanity. The Holy Prophet was, in the words of Qur'an, the "mercy for all the worlds" (21:107).

Muslims everywhere celebrate this occasion with great rejoicing. Again, this is not an occasion for frivolity or pleasure-seeking, but an occasion of inner joy and happiness. Assemblies are held throughout the Muslim world to narrate the stories of the Prophet's birth, childhood, manhood, his preaching, his character, his sufferings and his forgiveness of even his most bitter enemies, his fortitude in the face of general opposition, his emigration to Medina, his treatment of others, his leadership in battle, and his final triumph, through God's grace, over the hearts of men.

The 12th of Rabi' al-Awwal is not the only day on which the birthday of the Prophet (peace be on him) is celebrated; rather the whole month of Rabi' al-Awwal is celebrated as the "birth month" of the Prophet.

"God and His angels bless the Prophet. O you who believe! (You too) bless him and salute him with a worthy salutation." (33:56)

(c) *Lailat Al-Qadr* (The Night of Power)

The night in which Prophet Muhammad (peace be on him) first received the message from God communicated by the Angel Gabriel is referred to in Qur'an as 'The Night of Power' *(Lailat al-Qadr).* Muhammad was then forty years old. The first verses which Gabriel recited to him on that night were the following:

"Read, in the name of thy Sustainer, Who created — created man from a clot. Read, and thy Sustainer is the Most Bountiful One, Who taught the use of the pen — taught man that which he did not know." (961:1-5)

The communication of the Qur'an to Prophet Muhammad (peace be on him) continued during the twenty-three years of his messengership and ended shortly before his death with the fourth verse of the fifth chapter (see Unit 9: Qur'an and Hadith).

There is no reliable way to be sure which night of Ramadan is *Lailat al-Qadr,* but we do know from sound *hadiths* (traditions of the Prophet) that it is one of the odd-numbered nights of the last ten days of Ramadan. In some Muslims countries, the night of 27th of Ramadan — that is, the night preceding the twenty-seventh day — is observed as *Lailat al-Qadr.* In Qur'an it is said about this Night:

"We have indeed revealed this (Qur'an) in the Night of Power. And what will make thee understand what the Night of Power is? The Night of Power is better than an thousand months. Therein descend the angels and the Spirit [Gabriel] by God's permission, on every errand. Peace — until the day breaks." (97:1-5)

A portion of the night on which *Lailat al-Qadr* is observed ought to be spend in reading Qur'an, in supererogatory or additional prayer (*salat*) and supplication. In fact, the whole month of Ramadan is dedicated to fasting, prayer, charity and goodwill (see Unit 4: Fasting). 'Aisha, the Prophet's wife, reported that God's messenger Muhammad (peace be on him) used to exert himself in devotion during the last ten nights of Ramadan to a greater extent than at any other time.

(d) *Lailat al-Isra wa al-Mi'raj* (The Night of the Journey and the Ascension

During the tenth year of his prophethood, in the night of 27th Rajab, the Holy Prophet (peace be on him) saw, in a most radiant vision — physical as well as spiritual — some of the signs of God. Qur'an refers to this experience in the following verses:

"Glory be to Him Who did take His servant [Muhammad] for a journey by night from the Sacred Mosque [Ka'aba] to the Farthest Mosque [the remains of Solomon's Temple in Jerusalem] — the precincts of which We have blessed — that We might show him some of Our signs. He is the All-Hearing, the All-Seeing." (17:1)

Through this manifestation, God raised the Prophet (peace be on him) to the highest spiritual elevation of which man is capable. During this night the five daily prayers (*salat*) were prescribed by God. Muslims celebrate this night by reading Qur'an and praying supererogatory (additional) prayers.

1. *Aqd Nikah* (The Marriage Contract)

The Islamic teachings encourage Muslims to marry, to live together in mutual love, harmony and respect, to have children and to raise them as believing and practicing Muslims. Marriage in Islam is a civil contract, a mutual agreement of two persons before God and man, and no mystical or sacramental significance is associated with it.

Since there is no priesthood in Islam, it is not required — although it is desirable for the sake of giving a form to the ceremony of marriage itself — to have a person officiating between the bride and groom. It is necessary only that at least two adult Muslims be present to witness the exchange of vows and that the event be announced and made known publicly. This is the minimum requirement according to Islamic law. However, customarily the wedding date is announced beforehand and the ceremony is attended by relatives and friends of two parties. This may be done in any appropriate manner, with as little or much ceremony and embellishment as desired. keeping in mind that we are enjoined by God in Qur'an not to make displays of wealth to impress others and that we are not to be wasteful.

The ceremony may be performed at any convenient and appropriate gathering place. Some person known for his knowledge of Islamic law ordinarily officiates for the exchange of marriage vows. He may recite some passages from Qur'an *(al-Fateha* and *Surah* 28, verses 22-28, are suitable for this occasion) and give a general discourse on the social and religious significance of marriage, the responsibilities and rights of the husband and wife, and pray for God's blessing on the newly-married couple. The following, or its equivalent, is a possible wording of the exchange of vows:

The Bride groom: "I,________________, take you,________
The Bride:

daughter of ________________________________

son of ________________________________, as my lawfully married wife/husband before God and before the present company, in accordance with the precepts of Qur'an and

167

Sunnah. I pledge to do my utmost to render this marriage an act of obedience to God, to make it a relationship of mutual love, mercy, peace, faithfulness and co-operation. Let God be my witness, for God is the best of all witnesses. Amen."

Apart from verbal exchanges of the pledges, both the bride and groom sign a written contract of which three copies should be prepared, before the witnesses, and at least two witnesses sign the document. One copy is filed with the nearest civil court (in a Muslim country) and the other copies may be retained by each of the two partners. (In this country, of course, certain other requirements are to be satisfied for a legal marriage.)

It is required by Qur'an that a man give to his wife some type of marriage gift (*mehr*). This sum of money, property or other type of gift is hers by right, and her husband may not claim it at any time. If a divorce, for which provision is made in Islamic law, takes place, the husband must pay this sum to his wife, unless she voluntarily decides to forgo the whole or part of it; and if he dies, the amount of the *mehr* is turned over to the wife from his property before any other settlements are made, if it has not already been paid to her. Otherwise, however, the payment may be made by mutual agreement over a period of time. The nature of the gift and the method of payment should be specified at the time of marriage and incorporated into the marriage contract. This marriage gift may take the form of a sum of money, property, education given to the wife, or something else of value. A story is related concerning a Muslim who came to the Prophet (peace be on him), saying that he was too poor to have any gift to give to his intended wife. The Prophet asked if he knew any part of Qur'an. When the man replied that he did the Prophet instructed him to teach it to his wife as his marriage gift to her.

While in some religions marriage between cousins is not allowed, it is permitted in Islam. Qur'an 4:22-24 mentions the relationships between whom marriage is prohibited. Muslim men are permitted to marry Christian or Jewish women, as Qur'an says:

"And (lawful to you) in marriage are chaste women who are believers, and chaste women from among the People of the Book

[Jews and Christians], revealed before your time — provided you give them their marriage gift, taking them in honest wedlock, not in fornication, nor as secret love-companions." (5:6)

2. Birth

The birth of a baby is a time for rejoicing. A Muslim looks upon his child as a gift and a trust from God. In some Muslim countries, the choosing of a name for the infant is a special occasion, usually celebrated on the seventh day after birth. Relatives and friends gather at the home of the parents, and after the recitation of some passages from Qur'an, the name is announced by the father. A feast follows.

It is *sunnah* (the practice) of Prophet Muhammad, who followed the *sunnah* of Prophet Abraham (peace be on them), to circumcise male infants. In this country, this minor operation can be done routinely in the hospital within a few days of the child's birth.

It is also Sunnah to shave the baby's head on the seventh, fourteenth or twenty-first day after birth and to distribute charity among the poor on this occasion.

3. Death

Death is the end of the present life, but a Muslim believes in the life Hereafter. For Muslims, then, death is not the final end, but a temporary separation from the beloved person, who will be brought back to life on the Day of Judgment and, if God wills, reunited with his family once more. Although, we mourn the loss of our relative or friend, we do not indulge in extravagant expressions of grief like wailing or loud crying. This is an offense against God's will. When we first hear the news of a person's death, we say:

"Inna li Allah wa inna ilaihe raji'un."

"Verily, unto God do we belong and, verily, unto Him shall we return." (2:156)

Relatives and friends gather at the home of the deceased person, give comfort and solace to the immediate family members, recite Qur'an, and pray for God's forgiveness and mercy for the dead.

The Holy Prophet (peace be on him) strongly urged Muslims to bury the dead without delay. For burial, the body is washed (a man by men and a woman by women), wrapped in one or two sheets of clean white cloth, put on a cot or stretcher (a coffin may be used), and carried on the shoulders of men to a mosque or to the burial place itself for the funeral prayer *(salat al-janazah)*.

This prayer is a common obligation *(fard kifayah)* on Muslims, meaning that it should be observed by at least a few but not necessarily by all who are associated with the event. The funeral prayer is offered in congregation and does not have any bowing *(ruku')* or prostration *(sujud)*. It consists of four *takbirs* (recitations, of *"Allahu Akbar"* — God is Most Great). Praise (Thana) and the opening chapter of Qur'an (Al-Fateha) are recited after the first *takbir;* the Ibrahimi prayer after the second *takbir;* a prayer for the dead, for oneself and for others in any suitable words or language, said silently, after the third *takbir;* and the peace greetings (*"Assalamu alaikum wa rahamat Ullah"*) after the fourth *takbir.*

The body is then buried.

"All that is on earth will perish, and there will remain only the Face of thy Sustainer, majestic, full of bounty and honor."
(55:26-27)

BASIC PRINCIPLES

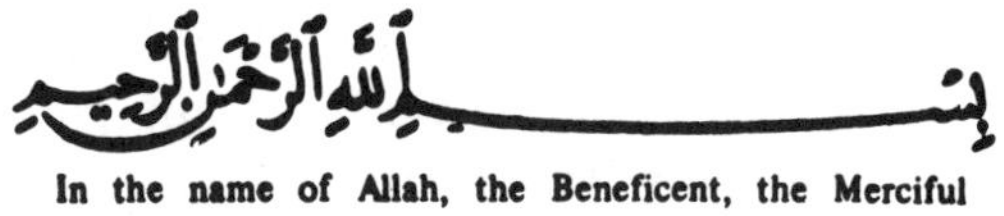

In the name of Allah, the Beneficent, the Merciful

DIRECTIONS FOR THE USE OF THIS UNIT:

Each of the boxes on the following pages is referred to as a frame. Each frame gives you information about Islam which you will use in making a response. The small box on the left of the large box is the answer column.

Now turn to page 1. Cover the answer column with a piece of paper. Read the first frame. You will find a space has been left for you to fill in. Most responses can be made orally; some you will prefer to write. In either case, check each of your answers with the correct answer next to the information frame in the answer column.

Then go to the next frame. Read it, give your answer, and check your answer by uncovering the correct answer. When you turn to a new page, try to avoid looking at the answers. Cover them before you begin reading the first frame.

At the end of the unit is a question sheet. Use it to check your progress and retention. You will find this introductory unit very helpful to you as your start your course about Islam.

Islam	Islam is the name given to our religion. The word _____________ means submission, obedience, commitment and peace in Arabic.
submit, obey commit	Submission means we should cheerfully accept and act upon God's commandments. Obedience means we follow God's law. Commitment means we bind ourselves to God; we put ourselves in His charge. If we _________ to God's Will, _________ His laws, and _______ ourselves to His charge, we will have peace.
peace	We will experience peace within ourselves and with other people, as well as _____________ on earth.
God	Islam teaches that there is only One God, that God is One. Believing in _____________ is the basis and foundation of Islam. The Arabic name for God is Allah.
Sustainer	God is the Creator and Sustainer of the universe. God is the Creator and _____________ of man. God has given us life and all things in the world.
God	_____________ is Most Merciful, Most Just, Most Wise. His Will is a will of kindness and goodness. The law He made for us is best for us.
Islam	Islam is the religion of truth and righteousness. It is not a new religion. Islam was ordained by God. _____________ has always been and will be until the end of time.
Muslim	A person who holds the beliefs and follows the practices of Islam is called a _____________.

God	Muslims worship ___________ alone. A Muslim believes, "There is no god except GOD."
Muslim	God has no partner. He is the Only One, so a ___________ always turns to God and to no else for help and guidance.
God	A Muslim asks ___________ for help. God helps a Muslim by giving him good ideas. When a Muslim turns to God for guidance, he knows that he has turned to the Only One Who is Supreme and Powerful.
God	All good things in our lives come in some way from ___________ . We should thank God because He provides for us and because He guides us.
merciful	God is ___________ . The day, the night, the sun, the moon, the stars, the rain, the trees, the entire earth, were all given to us through God's mercy for our use and enjoyment.
messenger	A Muslim believes in all the messengers and prophets of God. Abraham was among the first prophets. Moses was a messenger. Jesus Christ was a messenger. Muhammad was the last ___________ of God.
prophet	A messenger is a ___________ to whom God reveals a Scripture or a Book.
messenger	God revealed the Holy Qur'an to Muhammad. Therefore he is both a prophet and a ___________ .
God	These messengers or prophets were men chosen by ___________ to deliver His Divine

God messengers	**message and to teach mankind. Because God is merciful, He does not hold any person responsible until He has shown him the right** way. This is why __________ has sent many ________________ and prophets.
God messengers	The Divine message of __________ was sent to us through these _______________ through the ages. Some parts of these messages were preserved in writing.
revelation	The original Jewish Torah and the original Christian Gospel were both revealed by God. The Holy Qur'an is the last ____________ from God to mankind, for as long as it remains intact, just as it was revealed, there is no need for any other revelation.
Holy Qur'an	The ________________________ was revealed by God to Muhammad (peace be on him), the last Prophet, through the Angel Gabriel.
Holy Qur'an	After the other collections of the word of God were lost or changed, the ____________ was revealed to Muhammad. The Qur'an was revealed in Arabic from God, sentence by sentence at different times over a period of twenty-three years.
Holy Qur'an	The _________________ is the only original, real and complete Book of God's revelation left to us. The Holy Qur'an is the only scripture in human history preserved in its complete and original form without any change in style, wording or punctuation.
Traditions of **Muhammad**	The Holy Qur'an is the word of God. The ____________________ are practical interpretations of the Qur'an. The Tradi-

174

tions of Muhammad are called *Hadith* in Arabic.

Hadith	____________ includes the recorded sayings and deeds of the Prophet. It also includes deeds of the Prophet's companions which had his approval.
Hadith, the Traditions of Muhammad Holy Qur'an	Muhammad showed us by his life the way to practice the laws and injunctions God gave us in the Qur'an. We can know about his words and deeds by reading ____________, __________________________, which were reported by his companions. This too is a guide for us as well as an interpretation of the _______________ .
Muslim	A true __________ believes in the angels of God. Angels are creatures of God whose nature is purely spiritual.
angels	You can feel the movement of the wind sometimes, and you can often see the results of this movement. You know the wind is there, but you cannot see it. Similarly you know that the __________ are there, but you cannot see them.
God	These angels obey __________ . There are many of them and each one has his work to do.
Muslims	__________ believe that there are more things in the universe than just what we can perceive with our five senses.
Muslims God	__________ believe in the Day of Judgment. The Master of the Day of Judgment is __________ .
God	Someday, when __________ decides, an

God

end will come to this world. The dead will rise from their graves. On that day we will have to look at all the things we did in our life, both good and bad. We will be rewarded for our good deeds and punished for our bad deeds as ______________ in His infinite knowledge, justice and mercy sees fit to punish or reward us.

Muslims

God

______________ believe in Heaven and Hell, but the real nature of Heaven and Hell cannot be known to us. Only ______________ knows their real nature.

Holy Qur'an

The ______________ does give us descriptions of Heaven and Hell, but these descriptions only represent Heaven and Hell. God told us about Heaven and Hell, which we cannot really know about, in the only way we can grasp, by putting these descriptions in word pictures we understand.

Muslims

______________ believe that God is constantly active and concerned with His creation.   As God is Merciful, Beneficent and Wise, everything He does has a good motive and purpose.

God's

God's

Although we often fail to understand God's purposes, yet we accept His plans. We must remember that our thinking in limited, while ______________ is limitless. We must do all within our power to make this a better world and have faith that all we cannot control is ______________ will.

Muslims

God

______________ believe that life is meaningful, and that the purpose of life is to worship and serve ______________ .

obey

God

To worship God means more than prayer. It means to love Him, to ________________ His commandments and to do what is right. ________________ expects each of us to do our best with our lives.

Muslims

actions

________________ believe that man is born free from sin. We come into this world with freedom to do either good or evil. By the time we become adults we are held responsible for our actions. Each person is responsible to God for his own ________________ .

---

good

Muslims believe that human nature is more likely to be ________________ than evil. The fact that God cares for man and helps him proves that man is capable of doing good and being responsible for his own actions.

God

Muslims believe that each man must strive toward what is good through the guidance of ________________ . In order to gain the good of the next world as well as a better life on this earth, each Muslim must combine faith and action, belief and practice.

Holy Qur'an

faith

But faith must come through rational thinking. The teachings of the ________________ are based on reason. Islam is based on natural convictions and ________________ , and should not be forced on anyone.

---

righteousness
God

In the second Surah, Verse 177, of the Qur'an, God tells us: "It is not righteousness that you turn your faces toward the East or the West; but it is ________________ — to believe in ________________ and the Last Day, and the Angels, and the Book, and the Messengers; to spend of your substance, out of love for Him, for your kin, for orphans, for the needy, for

prayer	the wayfarer, for those who ask, and for the ransom of slaves; to be steadfast in __________, and practice regular charity; to fulfill the contracts which you have made; and to be
patient	firm and __________________, in pain (or suffering) and adversity, and throughout all periods of panic. Such are the people of truth, the God-fearing."
wealth	God asks us in this verse to give our __________, for His sake, to those in need, whether they are our relatives, our friends, or strangers.
money	Helping others means not only to give our __________________, but also our abilities, our time, our energies whenever and wherever we can. After all, money is only a small part of what God has given us to spend.
worship	God also asks us in this verse to be regular in prayer and to pay the poor-due. Prayer, of course, is a form of worship, but we also __________________ God when we think of Him. We worship God when we do an act of kindness for His sake, when we fulfill our obligations and when we strive toward what is right and avoid what is wrong.
Islam	Prayer is one of the five pillars of __________. Muslims observe the first prayer early in the morning between the time the first light becomes visible and a few minutes before
prayer	sunrise. We call this early morning __________ *Fajr*. *Fajr* means "dawn" in Arabic.
prayer	Our second prayer is observed between noon and mid-afternoon. This time of __________ is called *Dhur*, which means "noon."
prayer	Our third __________________ , *'Asr*, extends from

mid-afternoon until a few minutes before sunset. *'Asr* means "afternoon."

---

prayer

Our fourth ___________, *Maghrib*, is observed just after sunset until the last light fades. *Maghrib* means "sunset."

---

prayer

Our fifth ___________, *'Isha,* is observed at some time during the night until dawn begins to break. *'Isha* means "evening."

Remember that God does not need man's prayer, for He is free from all needs. We pray for our own spiritual improvement, to remember God at all times, and to glorify Him. When we ___________ regularly we become better ___________ and better human beings.

pray
Muslims

---

needy

God asks us to give charity to those who are ___________ . We should give our money to individuals or organizations, but we are also giving charity when we help an old person across the street or comfort a crying child. We have given ___________ when we share our food with others or show politeness to a stranger.

charity

---

charity

It is well to remember that none of us get through life without receiving ___________ as well as giving it.

Qur'an

God tells us further in the same verse of ___________ (2:177) that it is part of righteousness "to fulfil the contracts which you have made; and to be firm and ___________, in pain (or suffering) and adversity, and throughout all periods of panic. Such are the people of truth, the God-fearing."

patient

Righteousness	In other words, we must make ourselves firm and unshakeable in all circumstances, no matter what happens. _______________ is not just what we say, but also what we do.
duties	Muslims are commanded by God to observe five specific duties. We call these _______________ the five pillars of Islam.
pillar God Muhammad	The first _______________ is the proclamation, "There is no deity except _______________ and _______________ is a messenger of God."
declaration	When this declaration of faith is made with sincerity, you are on the way to the Islamic way of life. If this _______________ is followed by action, then you are a Muslim.
pillar, prayer five	The second _______________ of Islam is regular _______________. A Muslim is required to observe prayers _______________ times a day.
pillar of Islam fasting	The third _______________ is fasting. A Muslim must observe the entire lunar month of *Ramadan* as a month of _______________. When a Muslim fasts, he neither eats, drinks, nor indulges other physical desires between dawn and sunset during this month.
pillar of Islam needy	The fourth _______________ is *Zakat* or poor-due. A Muslim must give at least two and one-half per cent of his savings each year as a poor-due to help the _______________ This can be given either to individuals or to organizations.
pillar of Islam	The fifth _______________ is *Hajj* or pilgrimage to Mecca. A Muslim should

180

God Mecca, Prophet	go once in his lifetime to perform a special visit to the Ka'aba in Mecca, if circumstances permit. The Ka'aba is the first house of worship of One _____________ , built many centuries ago in _____________ by the ___ _____________ Abraham and his son Ishmael.
proclamation, prayer, fasting, poor-due, pilgrimage	The five specific duties or pillars of Islam are: _____________ , _____________ _____________ , _____________ and _____________
Muslims	All these duties are intended to give _________ a feeling of closeness to God, a pattern of self-discipline, and a sense of the fellowship of all human beings regardless of color, race, nationality, language, or social status.
forbidden good	God has forbidden certain things, for He wishes to protect man from what is harmful. Sometimes we do not understand why certain things are _____________ , but if we remember that God knows what we do not know and that whatever God commands is for the _________ of man, we can accept these commands willingly.
drink	God has forbidden us the use of any kind of intoxicating _____________ or drug.
pork	God does not allow us to eat _____________ in any form.
birds of prey	God does not allow us to eat any _____________ , such as hawks, eagles, vultures, crows, or any reptile or rodent.
hurt	God orders us to avoid doing anything shameful or indecent which might _____________

	the mind, the soul or the body of ourselves and others.
good harmful	All wholesome and ______________ things are lawful for Muslims. God only forbids those things which are ______________ , and it is every Muslim's responsibility to know what things are forbidden.
obey	God asks us to ____________ His laws.
love	God asks us to ____________ Him and His messenger Muhammad.
private	God asks us to be sincere and steadfast to Him in ____________ as well as in public.
be kind	God asks us to ________________ to our parents, our children, our relatives and all human beings.
just	God asks us to be fair and ___________ in all our dealings with others, even if we ourselves are at fault.
reliable	God asks us to be sincere, honest, decent, truthful, trustworthy and ______________ .
appearance behavior	God asks us to be modest in our __________ and virtuous in our ________________ .
keep	God asks us to ___________ our promises.
visit comfort	God asks us to help the needy, ___________ the sick, and ________________ the distressed.
patience, courage	God asks us to have ________________ and ________________ in all times of distress and suffering.

182

tolerance forgiveness	God asks us to show ______________ toward others and to practice ____________ and humility.
control	God asks us to ____________ our anger.
peace	God asks us to make ____________ between people.
avoid	God asks us to ____________ gossiping, meddling, spying, slandering, speaking evil of others or being suspicious.
knowledge	God asks us to seek ____________ .
debts	God asks us to take care of our obligations and to pay back our ____________ .
help	God asks us to do good in all ways and to ____________ others to do good also.
strive evil	God asks us to ____________ hard toward righteousness and to fight against ________ .
faith trust	God asks us to have ____________ and ____________ in Him at all times and under all circumstances.
right	God asks us to be firm in our stand for what is ________ .
community	God asks us to be responsible and law-abiding members of our ____________ or nation.
justice kindness	God asks us to accept and practice ________ and ____________ among all men.

Compiled and prepared by Jane Beck Smith.

Cut on dotted line and hang up for easy reference

THE FIVE DAILY PRAYERS

Name of Prayer	Timing	Number of *Rakats*	First Two *Rakats*-- Aloud or Silent	*Additional (Sunnah) Prayers* Number of *Rakats* Before Obligatory *(Fard)* Prayer	Number of *Rakats* After Obligatory *(Fard)* Prayer
Fajr	Between dawn until just before sunrise	2	Aloud	2	None
Dhur	Between just past noon and mid-afternoon	4	Silent	2 or 4	2
'Asr	Between mid-afternoon until just before sunset	4	Silent	None, or 2 or 4	None
Maghrib	Between just after sunset until almost dark	3	Aloud	None	2
'Isha	Between dark and shortly before dawn	4	Aloud	None	2 plus 3